MY NAME IS TANI...

AND I BELIEVE IN MIRACLES

MY NAME IS TANI...

AND I BELIEVE IN MIRACLES

THE AMAZING TRUE STORY OF ONE BOY'S JOURNEY
FROM REFUGEE TO CHESS CHAMPION

TANI ADEWUMI

with Kayode and Oluwatoyin Adewumi

and Craig Borlase

W PUBLISHING GROUP

AN IMPRINT OF THOMAS NELSON

Published in Nashville, Tennessee, by W Publishing Group, an imprint of Thomas Nelson.

Thomas Nelson titles may be purchased in bulk for educational, business, fund-raising, or sales promotional use. For information, please e-mail SpecialMarkets@ThomasNelson.com.

Any Internet addresses, phone numbers, or company or product information printed in this book are offered as a resource and are not intended in any way to be or to imply an endorsement by Thomas Nelson, nor does Thomas Nelson vouch for the existence, content, or services of these sites, phone numbers, companies, or products beyond the life of this book.

The names and identifying details of some individuals discussed in this book have been changed to protect their privacy.

ISBN 978-0-7852-3271-1 (HC)
ISBN 978-0-7852-3274-2 (e-Book)

Library of Congress Control Number: 2019952508

Printed in the United States of America
20 21 22 23 24 LSC 10 9 8 7 6 5 4 3 2 1

To almighty God, the Alpha and Omega, the beginning and the end.
To my dad, my mom, and my brother.
And to the whole world.
Thank you!

CONTENTS

Prologue ix

PART 1: When Danger Knocks 1

PART 2: Searching for Home 37

PART 3: Hope Restored 73

PART 4: Generous People 113

PART 5: Blessed 161

Acknowledgments 203

Notes 205

About the Authors 207

PROLOGUE

My name is Tani, and my family says I like to ask a lot of questions. They're right. I like puzzles. I like riddles. I like trying to figure out why things happen and how things work.

But things have been different lately. Instead of asking the questions, I've been the one trying to answer them. A lot of people have wanted to know all kinds of things about me and my life. They want to know what life was like for me and how I feel about the way things have changed. They want me to tell my story, and I want to tell it, but there's never enough time to say everything that's in my head.

So this book is going to be my answer.

But if I'm going to tell you my story, I need to start by saying that I don't remember much about Nigeria. I know that I was six years old when these really bad people called Boko Haram tried to kill my dad and we had to leave—but honestly, I was asleep most of the times they came looking for my dad, so you'd have to ask him about that.

What I do remember about life in Nigeria is playing soccer and my brother, Austin, trying to teach me chess and how one day I was watching the news on the TV and there was this airplane pilot who had just done something amazing. He was Nigerian like me, and there must have been a really serious problem with the plane because everyone was excited about the fact that he had landed safely and everyone survived. From that moment on

I wanted to be a pilot. It's not because of money, though. Being a pilot makes you rich, but I don't mean *money* rich. I liked the idea of doing something like that to help people.

I remember *a lot* about life in America. Like how when we moved to New York I learned about chess, properly this time, and discovered that the very best players in the world are called grand masters, and so, from then on, I started to think that it might be good to be a grand master too. And then one day Coach Shawn Martinez actually took me to meet Fabiano Caruana, who is the number two chess player in the *whole world*! He shook my hand and we talked, and from that moment on, I decided that I definitely wanted to be a grand master.

And then something happened.

I won a chess competition, and lots and lots and lots of people wanted to talk to me. It wasn't just people from New York or even America. People from all over the world wanted to know my story. Some of them still do.

A lot of the people I have spoken to ask me about chess. They say things like "How has chess changed your life?" or "What do you like most about playing chess?" I mostly give them the same answer to both questions, which is that chess has taught me how to do deep thinking. Sometimes people laugh when they hear me say that, but I don't see how it's very funny.

The more I think about all this, the more I know that I can't answer either of those questions quickly. I need a lot more than one minute to be able to explain everything. And I don't think I can even do it all myself because there's so much that I don't remember.

So the best way to tell my story is to have my parents help me. They know all the details of everything that's happened, and they're also my heroes. None of this would've even happened if it hadn't been for them.

I would have asked Austin to help tell this story, too, but he likes basketball a lot more than he likes writing. But he's still my hero as well.

After I won the chess tournament and spoke to all those people, life changed really quickly for all of us. Recently I've been thinking again about being a pilot. Since talking to everyone, I now know that there are a lot of places I've not been to, and if I were a pilot, maybe I could go see them. I could fly to China, Japan, Arizona, Kentucky, Turkey, and England. I want to go to these places and live there for maybe one whole year or maybe just five months. I read in a book that the average person lives to be seventy-one years old, but I think I'm not going to live the average. I think I'm going to live to be more than one hundred. So maybe I'll do both—be a grand master and a pilot too. I'd like that.

I don't know what I'm going to be. My dad says that's okay.

But I do know this much. I believe in miracles.

PART 1
WHEN DANGER KNOCKS

1 | THE DAY SCHOOL CLOSED EARLY

TANI ——————

At first I was happy when they sent us home from school early. I think I was in first grade and it was before Christmastime. What I know for sure is that after morning recess the teachers told us school was done for the day and that we should leave.

Wow. That was good news.

You would have thought the teachers would have been happy about getting out of school early, too, but they weren't. They all looked serious as they whispered together. They hurried us out into the yard and stood watching us, making sure we stayed behind the locked gates until our parents came to fetch us.

Austin and I had to wait for *ages* until Mom came, but it didn't matter. We were still happy. Austin even let me sit next to him on the bench.

And when we got home, we played soccer in the courtyard with some friends.

Soccer is not an easy game when you're little and you're playing your big brother and his friends who are way taller than you. And it's really hard when they don't pass you the ball, even though you stand on the side and wave your arms and shout over and over to them, "Hey, pass me the ball! I'm over here! Pass it to me! Pass it!"

They just ignored me. I shouted louder, but they still ignored me. Then, even though I really didn't want to, I started to cry. I couldn't stop the tears.

So that was when a really good day stopped being so good after all.

I went inside and saw Mom. Granddad was there too. They both looked as serious as the teachers looked. I didn't like the fact that I was crying, but I was really upset about the soccer game. I told Mom about Austin and his friends not passing the ball to me, and she said she'd go speak to them. But she didn't. She just gave me a hug while she kept talking with Granddad about the school closing early.

I was only half listening, but when Granddad asked, "How long is it closed for?" and Mom said, "I don't know," I sat up.

I asked, "What do you mean? Is there school tomorrow?"

Mom shook her head and said, "It's closed for a while. Just until . . ."

She didn't finish her sentence. I didn't mind. I was running outside again, ready to tell the others this great news.

The rest of the day was good. Really good. Everyone was so happy about school being closed, and for a long time I played soccer, and they even passed the ball to me *four times*. I didn't score any goals, but it was still fun.

Later, when our friends had gone and it had gotten dark and the power hadn't cut out for once, we were all in the living room. Austin was doing his homework, and Mom and Dad were watching the TV news. I don't really like TV too much, so I was probably playing or reading or something like that.

The man on TV said a word that made me stop whatever I was doing and listen. It was a word that I had heard for the first time earlier that day.

When Dad quickly turned off the TV, I said, "Dad, what's bokoharam?"

He only looked at me for a really short time and then did the thing he does where he frowns and shakes his head. When he does that it always reminds me of someone trying to shake a fly from his face without using his hands. He said, "It is nothing that you need to worry about. Why do you ask?"

And I said, "It's what the teachers were all talking about today before they sent us home. Is it like Christmas? Is that why they've closed the school?"

He looked at Mom then back at me. He spoke in a very serious way. "No. I tell you, Tani, this is not something you should worry about. And it's bedtime now."

When Dad sends us to bed, there's no point arguing. So I went straight-away. Whatever bokoharam was, I liked it. Hopefully there would be some more of it soon so that we would get even more time off from school.

2 | FEAR IN A FLASH DRIVE

OLUWATOYIN ————————

Kayode, my husband, knows very little about chess. But he knows all about sacrifice. He knows that sometimes you must be willing to lose something precious in order to protect what you hold closest to your heart. He knows what it is to face an opponent who is ruthless, brutal, and hungry for your destruction. And he knows that in life there are moments when the only way to make it through to the victory that lies ahead is to be prepared to stand and fight until the very last breath.

It all started on what I thought was an ordinary day—an ordinary December day in the Nigerian capital city of Abuja. I had returned home from my job at the bank at around four in the afternoon, collecting Austin and Tani from school on the way. They were playing soccer in the courtyard with friends while I spent a final few hours with my father, who had been staying with us for two weeks and was due to return home to his wives that day.

That's right, his *wives*. As was the custom for many Muslim men of his age in Nigeria, my father was a polygamist, with four wives and one mistress. I know this sounds strange to an American reader, but he really was a great husband to all of the women he lived with and a great father to every single one of his twenty children. He was loyal to his faith and attended the mosque, but he was no fanatic. As his daughters, we were cultural Muslims more than religious ones. So when I, like all of my sisters, fell in love with a Christian man and told my father that I was going to be baptized, he did not discriminate or complain at all. He simply gave us the freedom to choose who we wanted to marry, and he continued to treat each and every one of us with the same love and kindness that he had always shown.

My father and I stood in the kitchen, smiling at the sounds that drifted on the hot breeze flowing in from outside. It was the same story every time Austin, Tani, and their friends played soccer. Apart from the occasional crash as the ball hit the metal fence, the loudest noise was Tani shouting over and over for someone to pass him the ball.

Like many five-year-old boys, when Tani decided to do something, he threw every ounce of himself into it. And like his peers, he struggled when he could not bend other people to his will. So, eventually, as was custom, Tani came into the kitchen.

"They won't pass it to me," he complained. "I tried doing what you said and asked them for the ball, but they didn't listen. Why don't they pass?"

This is Tani's difference from other kids. He asks more questions than any person I have ever met. When he finds something in life that interests him but that he doesn't understand, he simply will not rest until his curiosity is satisfied. And if you ever give him an answer that he tests and finds faulty, you can be sure that he'll be back with more questions.

I was about to try to answer his soccer questions when I heard the front door open, and my husband came in and greeted us all.

Kayode—whose name rhymes with *coyote*—was supposed to be in a rush. He had a meeting in the old capital city, Lagos, early the next morning, and he had planned to make the short flight from Abuja that evening. So I was surprised when Kayode—after he finished talking to Tani about the art of getting people to cooperate in a team sport and sent him back out to play—sat down at the table, pulled out his laptop, and plugged in a flash drive.

"Four men came to the shop this afternoon," he said when he saw me looking at him questioningly. "They want twenty-five thousand posters printed."

"Eh," I said, nodding. Kayode's printing business was thriving, and it was not unusual for an order of this size to come out of nowhere like this. Even so, I was thankful. With thirteen staff members at the shop, Kayode needed a steady flow of business to keep things healthy.

Only, Kayode suddenly did not look so healthy. He was sitting, frozen, staring at the screen.

"What is it?" I asked.

He tilted his head up toward me but his eyes stayed wide, locked on the screen. "Look," he said, spinning the laptop around, before calling for my father to come and join us.

Even though I could not read it properly, I recognized the Arabic writing immediately. Worse, though, was the logo beneath it—two AK-47s on either side of a thick book with a black-and-white flag flying over the top. There was not a single person in Nigeria at the time who would not have recognized it.

I stared at Kayode. He confirmed my fears with a nod as my father joined us. And while Kayode and I had been quiet, my father immediately raised his voice. "What are you doing working for people like this, son?"

"Dad, I am not working for them," he said. "Four men just came to the shop this afternoon. I have never met them before in my life. Can you read it?"

"Of course I can read it. It says, 'No to Western Education,' and 'Kill All Christians.' And you know who they are, don't you? You recognize the logo?"

"Boko Haram."

We stayed silent for the longest time. Even if Tani were complaining to his brother outside, I don't think we would have heard him. Fear had drained all sound from the room.

Eventually it was my father who spoke. "What are you going to do?"

My husband comes from a long line of wise and noble men. There is royalty in his ancestry, and he built a successful business out of nothing in just a few years. When we lived in Nigeria, his opinion was widely sought by friends and colleagues throughout the city, and he always knew what to do.

He was one of the few people on the planet who could answer Tani's questions. But for the first time that I could ever remember, Kayode Adewumi was lost. He was silent. He looked fearful.

He pulled the flash drive out of his laptop and put it in his pocket. "I have to go now."

3 | A DANGEROUS DILEMMA

KAYODE ——————————

When my wife and I named our sons, we chose carefully. Our firstborn, Austin, was named Adesina. It means "God opens doors to us." The world now knows our second son as Tani, but Tanitoluwa means "Who is like God?"

When we chose them, we wanted names that reflected the way we saw the world. We had no idea how significant those names would become.

I did not rest well the night I flew to Lagos. From the moment I plugged the flash drive into my laptop at home and opened the poster file, I was robbed of all peace.

I was not alone. Oluwatoyin felt the same way. So did her father.

"Kayode," he said as I put my laptop in my bag, "son, you should have nothing more to do with this job. Forget they ever visited you."

"But they have an appointment to see me tomorrow when I get back from Lagos."

"Then have your secretary cancel it."

"They did not leave a number."

"Then shut your shop for the day."

"They will come back."

"Then do not go to work tomorrow and have your secretary tell them you are unavailable when they arrive. She can tell them you are sick. You know what these men are like. They are killers, and now that you know their plans, have seen their faces, and can easily identify them, they will make you a target. You must do everything possible to avoid them."

I understood why he was saying this. He knew better than I did how dangerous Boko Haram was. But I was not convinced that I could simply hide and hope to be left alone. "No, Dad," I said as I walked out to the car. "I must face them myself."

I had planned to use the short flight to Lagos to prepare my quotation for the job. As I sat on the plane, I had no pen in my hand, no piece of paper resting on the plastic tray in front of me, but I was thinking about the men and the poster all the same. And I was trying my best to calculate how I could remove myself from the equation and cause them to forget all about me.

Five hundred miles later I finally had a plan.

As soon as I landed, I put it into action. I phoned my shop manager and informed him not to start up any machines the next day. I told my secretary that when the four gentlemen who had visited earlier that day returned the next morning, she should show them straight into my office. And I told myself that this was the only way—that only by facing them myself would I be able to put an end to it.

After lying awake most of the night and then fighting the urge to be distracted during my seven o'clock meeting the next morning, I took the hour-long flight back to Abuja. I wanted to get to my shop quickly, but I was also dreading the moment the four men would arrive.

The moment I walked into the shop, it felt wrong. With thirteen people employed there, the whole place was usually full of sound. People would be laughing and calling out over the noise of the machines as they produced books, posters, and everything else.

But on that day in late December, there was nothing. No noise, no chaos. No laughter, no shouts. Just silence.

I had been careful not to tell my team about the previous day's visit—I did not want them letting their nerves or their fear take over—but they knew when I gave the order to turn everything off that something was wrong.

I talked a little with some of the team then went to my office. I wanted to be ready to receive the men. I did not want them in my shop a second longer than was absolutely necessary.

On the wall above my desk was a cross. It had always been there, and it was as important to me as the pictures of Oluwatoyin and the boys on my desk. But for a moment, I have to confess that I considered removing it. I wondered how wise it was to advertise that I was one of the very people whose death their poster was calling for. But what if they had seen it the day before and noticed that I had taken it down overnight? If that happened, they'd know for sure that I had looked at their poster and that I knew their secret. Besides, my father had always taught me well. "Know where you come from," he'd said so many times. "Never be ashamed of who you are. Hold yourself with dignity. Stand firm."

So I left the cross in place and waited.

10:30 A.M.

The time they were supposed to arrive. There was no sign of them.

I rehearsed what I was going to say. Over and over I said the words in my head, repeating them until they started to lose their meaning.

10:41 A.M.

Still nothing. I took the flash drive out of my pocket and placed it on the desk. I wanted it—and the men—gone as soon as possible.

I closed my eyes, but not because I was tired. Sleep was the last thing on my mind. But at least closing my eyes helped to distract me, if only for a few seconds.

10:43 A.M.

Nothing. I grabbed the flash drive and put it back in my pocket.

And then, from the other side of my door, I could hear voices. Deep and rich, those voices uttered their words sparingly. I knew even before my secretary opened my door and showed them in who was there—the same four men from yesterday. As before, there was a younger, smaller, smiling man who said little; an older, heavier man who did most of the talking; and two others who stood at the back and guarded the door.

I stood and offered the usual welcome for a morning visitor. I offered them a seat and some tea, inquired of their health, and asked if they had slept well.

None of them wanted to sit, to drink, or to talk.

As before, the larger man spoke first. "Do you have a price for us?"

I tried to adopt my most regretful smile. "I am sorry to tell you that I do not."

A glance passed between him and the smaller man. They both stiffened.

"The machines are broken," I said. "I am very sorry, but I—"

"Broken? How can you say that? We both heard them when we came yesterday."

"I know. They were working well, but they just died soon after you left. When we tried to turn them on this morning, nothing happened. We have called the engineers, but they have not even replied yet. It is going to be some time before we are able to print again."

They all stared at me.

"I am sorry," I said as I dug my hand into my pocket. "Of course, knowing that you want the job completed urgently and that I could not therefore assist you, I did not look at your flash drive. Here it is."

I placed the flash drive on my desk. The silence remained for some time. When it broke, it was the smaller man who spoke. His voice was hard, like iron. "You are stupid if you think we believe you! Your machines were working yesterday. We demand that you do the job!"

"Please," I said, trying my best to appear reasonable and sincere. "I'm a businessman. I like to make money. And I particularly like it when clients come to me without me having to go and look for the work. So to have you in here and my machines not working is a matter of great frustration for me. But what can I do? All I can suggest is that you visit some of the other shops farther down the road. There are plenty of them there, and they will all be happy to serve you."

I motioned to the door, but none of them moved.

I was stuck. I'd thought that I could be reasonable and convincing and create a little story that they could play along with. But I hadn't planned for this—to have four militant Islamic fanatics in my office, refusing to leave.

I needed to think of something, fast.

"Please," I said, my hands out wide, "come with me. I would like to show you something."

They looked wary, but they followed eventually.

"I don't usually let clients come back here," I said as I led them into the machine room, "but I want you to see for yourself. Look!"

I pointed out each of the machines and showed the blank screens and silent motors. I kept them clear of the main power switch that had been off since first thing that morning.

"Oh," I said, pulling my phone out of my pocket and pretending that a message had just arrived. "I need to deal with this. Wait here, please. I will be right back."

I slipped down beyond the machines at the end of the room, into the paper storage room, and out the back door, locking it silently behind me.

In the alley that ran behind my shop, I crouched down in the dust, behind the wall. When I was sure there was nobody around who could hear me, I made a genuine call on my phone.

"Hello?"

"Oluwatoyin, I am well," I said. I was surprised that I was out of breath.

"I hope you are not harmed. What happened?"

"I am well, thank God. I told them that the machines were broken and gave them the flash drive back. I said I had not looked at it and apologized."

"Did they believe you?"

I paused. I heard a car start up nearby.

"Kayode, where are you?"

"I am outside in the street around the back," I whispered. "When I told them that I could not take on their job, one of them flared up. He started shouting, saying that I was lying and that the machines were all working yesterday. I took them into the machine room and showed them that nothing was on, but I do not think they believed me."

"So how did you get them to leave?"

"I didn't. When they were talking together, I pretended that I had something to attend to, so I walked off and slipped out the back door. I think I just heard them leaving now. As soon as I close the shop, I will come home."

"Do you think it is settled?"

"With God's help, I hope so."

4 | UNWELCOME VISITORS

OLUWATOYIN ———————

Ever since a group of militants abducted 276 girls from a high school in northeast Nigeria in 2014, the whole world has known the name Boko Haram. As the Nigerian Taliban, the West African cousin of ISIS, Boko Haram's aim is to establish an Islamic state or caliphate in my homeland. Ruthless and wicked, Boko Haram fighters are the type of people who post videos online of men they have captured being decapitated. The kind of animals who do not just abduct schoolgirls but use many of them as suicide bombers.

As Nigeria's capital, Abuja has a long and bloody history with Boko Haram. There have been so many attacks that it is hard to keep count. But some are impossible to forget, like the 2011 bombing of the UN headquarters in the city that killed twenty-four people. Later that same year, on Christmas day, a Boko Haram suicide bomber detonated his vest in a packed church, killing almost forty. Another attack was used as cover for a prison break, while in 2015 there was a bomb blast so close to my office that I could feel the heat as I was hurried out onto the street by our security team. For days the hospitals were full of the injured and dying. For weeks we braced ourselves for the next attack, flinching at every siren, hating every loud and innocent bang.

Long before Kayode received his unwelcome visit, daily life in Abuja had changed because of Boko Haram's attacks. Every shopping mall and movie theater now had airport-style security. Our church had even started employing masked armed guards who would check every adult entering the building before each service.

We had no choice but to live with it. It became normal to see armed guards checking shopping carts or to pull your car over at a checkpoint. But every so often something happened to remind us that the threat was real and that it was ever increasing.

The day when the boys were sent home from school was precisely one of those times. Boko Haram had sent a message threatening to attack another school in the city, and as a result, the government decided to close all the schools. The boys were kept out for almost a whole week, and when they did return to the school gates—reluctantly, of course—they were not greeted by the usual cluster of teachers with bright smiles and clipboards but by soldiers with stern faces and machine guns.

Boko Haram was a pack of hyenas lurking in the shadows. With every attack they launched, they edged closer, and their snarls and growls grew louder. We had hoped that they would leave or that the government would somehow find a way to contain or even defeat them. But after Kayode came home with their flash drive, we knew that they were actively looking to publicize their intentions and flood the streets and mosques with thousands of posters stirring up hatred and inciting violence. We could no longer hide from the truth.

They were coming.

The only questions were how long it would be until they attacked and how close we would be to their target.

After they visited the printshop the second time and my husband escaped out the back, Kayode chose to work from home for a few days. I went to the bank as usual, taking the boys to school on the way. Part of me was nervous and felt the urge to panic every time I saw Kayode's name appear on my phone. But as the days passed and nothing dramatic happened, it became a little easier to tell myself that the threat had passed as well. Either the men had believed Kayode's lie or at least had decided to find a printer who was willing to help them.

Christmas passed by, and the new year began. Kayode returned to work, the boys resumed school, and life settled back into the usual rhythm.

I was at home one night watching a movie. It was dark already, the boys were asleep in their room, my father had returned to his home, and Kayode was meeting with a client at the Sheraton in town. When I heard a gentle knock on the front door, I checked the time.

Nine o'clock. Kayode must have forgotten his keys.

The second that I unlocked the door, it burst into me. Two men forced their way inside.

"Lie down!" shouted one of them. "Don't look up. Where is the pastor?"

Their question made no sense to me, but I was too terrified to speak. I covered my head with my hands, waiting for one of them to hit me, hoping that the boys stayed asleep.

One of the men came and stood beside me. I could see his shoes just beside my head.

"The pastor!" he hissed. His voice reminded me of broken glass. "Where is he?"

"I-I-I don't know any pastor here," I stammered. I could feel tears on my cheeks.

The other man started to search the living room, moving heavily as he opened drawers and threw things on the floor. I tried to keep track of him, knowing that as long as he was still in the room and the other one was right beside me, my boys might at least have a chance of staying safe.

The man beside me knelt down. I did not want to look at him directly, so I stared at the pistol that was right beside my face.

"Your husband," he said slowly, turning the gun so that it was pointing at me. "Where is he?"

When I spoke I did not recognize my own voice. It sounded so far away. "Not here."

"Where is his laptop?"

"With him."

He stood up and walked across the room. The sound of the other man searching stopped, and I listened as they talked. If they left the room and headed back toward the bedrooms, I would have to do something to distract them.

"What do we do now?"

"Use her as a message for her husband?"

Until then I'd been confused. Part of me had thought—hoped, even—that this was just a typical robbery. But when they started talking about the laptop and using me to send a message, I guessed it was something to do with the poster. And then when I heard one of them speak in Arabic, I had no doubt.

In that moment, kneeling on the floor, my hands cradling my head, fighting for breath, I wondered what type of message they might want to send Kayode. Might they be about to rape me? Kill me? Was this how I would end up, as one of those people whose death they videoed and posted online?

Out of nowhere I heard myself utter one of the few Arabic phrases that I remembered from my childhood. *"Atuasal 'iilayk*—'I'm begging you'!"

I wasn't sure if they would listen to me or understand what I was saying, but I carried on all the same. *"Atuasal 'iilayk. Atuasal 'iilayk. Atuasal 'iilayk."*

The shoes reappeared beside me. "Are you a Muslim?"

I did not hesitate for one second. The lie flowed from my mouth as freely as the tears from my eyes. "Yes! Yes! Yes, I am!"

The room fell silent. The shoes moved away from me.

"Let's go."

As soon as I heard the men leave, I ran to the door and locked it. I checked that the boys were still asleep, then searched for my phone among the pile of papers on the floor.

When Kayode picked up, I could hear the sound of the hotel bar in the background. I did not want to make him panic, but I wanted my husband home as soon as possible. So I told him as simply and calmly as I could that some men had come to the house looking for him. He asked me what they looked like. I had only received a glimpse of them as they burst through the door, but I tried my best.

"The bigger one pushed through the door, but it was the smaller one who had the gun."

"Where are they now?" I heard the fear enter his voice.

"Gone."

"Are they in the compound still?"

"I don't know. I have not left the house. Should I check?"

"No! Stay inside. I'm coming."

5 | LOOKING FOR A WAY OUT

KAYODE —————

I had left the hotel and was almost in my car before I ended my call with Oluwatoyin. I raced across the city, careful to avoid any checkpoints that might hold me up, and phoned her when I was around the corner from our home. She sounded a little calmer, but the closer I got to our gate, the more aware I was that they might still be lurking, lying in wait for me.

As soon as I was inside the house, Oluwatoyin burst into tears. She had started to clean up, but parts of the living room still lay in chaos. There were papers all over the floor and furniture was flipped over. It looked more like the work of ten men than two.

"The boys?" I asked.

"Asleep," she said, taking a deep breath. "I thought you gave them the flash drive back already?"

"I did. They must think I saved a copy on my laptop. Maybe they're worried we're going to tell the police."

"Should we?"

It was a good question. I wondered whether it would help at all. Boko

Haram had already attacked police stations and other facilities that were well guarded. One bomber had even been able to get inside a military barracks and slaughter soldiers at will. If we contacted the police, could they help us? And what if we contacted them and the news made it back to Boko Haram? Might we end up making the whole thing worse?

We decided that the best thing to do was to live as quietly as possible. For the rest of January, I kept the printshop closed and put an end to any late-night meetings with clients. I stayed at home as much as I could and was careful to check the street before Oluwatoyin left for work every day. With the added security at the boys' school, it seemed to both of us that they would be safer there than at home if the men ever decided to return. And we really did not want to worry the boys by changing their routine at all.

We counted the days and the weeks as they inched by. Every night when we climbed into bed, Oluwatoyin and I reminded each other that we were blessed to be alive, and the further we got from the night the men visited the house, the better we felt. Soon I found myself wondering again if the men had simply given up on me.

It was late one night when the boys were asleep and Oluwatoyin and I were watching something on TV—at least two months after the first visit to our home—that we heard the knocking at the door.

This time the knock was not the gentle tap that Oluwatoyin had described. It was angry and violent, as if whoever was on the other side was not trying to summon us to open the door but instead meant to force it off its hinges.

Oluwatoyin froze, staring at the door.

"Go to the boys' room," I said. "I will deal with them."

She looked at me. She opened her mouth to speak, but no words came. "Go!" I said. "It is me that they want. Let me face them. You go back there and pray."

The banging grew louder. Oluwatoyin hurried toward the back of the house, and I watched her ease open the boys' door and slip inside.

The banging carried on just as before. I knew the door was strong—in a wealthy neighborhood like ours, every home made security its priority—but the banging was so loud that I wondered how long it would hold.

I stood in front of the door. I did not know what I could do, but I knew that I needed to be there, to put myself between the two men and Oluwatoyin and the boys.

The banging paused. In the silence I thought I could hear Oluwatoyin's prayers.

Then the shouting began. The same two voices that I'd heard in my printshop. The same two who had been here before.

"We know you're in there!"

"Come outside!"

"We're going to take you!"

The banging on the front door resumed, even louder this time. I dropped to my knees and prayed.

I begged God not to make my wife a widow. I pleaded with Him not to let the men in. I prayed for the door to have supernatural strength. And I prayed that the men would leave.

The shouting and the banging continued. Minutes passed, and still I knelt on the floor in front of the door. I did not feel strong. I felt weak. I had no power to hold them back, and I tensed myself in anticipation that at any second the door would burst open, the cold night air would rush in, and they would drag me out.

But no such thing happened.

I carried on praying while they carried on banging and shouting.

And then, after a quarter hour, they stopped.

As quickly as it had begun, the banging ceased. I edged to the door and tried to work out if they were trying to trick me.

Nothing.

I waited, then edged to the window.

There was no sign of them. Just the sound of Oluwatoyin praying in the back.

The decision to leave our home and move away from the city was not a difficult one to make. After a few visits from the same men of Boko Haram, I had no doubt that they would return at some point in the future. And even though we had discussed going to the police each time, neither I nor Oluwatoyin felt at all confident that they would be able to protect us.

Leaving Abuja was our only option.

Our main concern was finding a way to leave that would not worry the boys. But when spring break was less than a week away, we made a plan. We would make the daylong drive southwest and stay in Akure, a tolerant, liberal city an hour south of my hometown, Ado Ekiti. It had a reputation for being safe and peaceful. Not as great a place to build a business as was Abuja, but a good place to hide from jihadis. Nobody would know us there, and we could either keep a low profile and stay away from everyone or make some day trips to spend time with family living nearby.

One of my closest friends found us a single-story home with a tall fence that we could rent for a few months, and we moved in. We agreed that if we liked it enough, we could gradually move our life down to Akure. We could find a good school for the boys, I could arrange for the printing equipment to be sent down and set up a new business, and Oluwatoyin might even be able to get a transfer to one of the local branches of the bank she worked for.

And for the first few days, everything went well. Abuja might as well have been a million miles away, and at times Boko Haram even felt like a distant memory or a dark nightmare from long ago. Soon I even noticed that Oluwatoyin and I were not panicking so much whenever anyone knocked on the front door.

It did not last.

6 | LEARNING A NEW GAME

TANI ————————

These are the things I liked about moving to the house with the tall fence.

We were near my uncle's house. He has a pool and I like swimming a lot, so Mom and Dad promised that we could go visit one day. We didn't, but I liked thinking about it all the same.

Austin let me have the bed by the window.

Mom did lots of cooking, and Austin and I got to help.

Mom and Dad were on vacation with us too. It wasn't like Mom never took a vacation—her job at the bank was good like that and let her take time off when we were not at school. But Dad never took vacations with us. He was always really busy with his work. So when we were in the house with the tall fence and we were all together as a family all the time, it was so good.

With none of our friends around to play soccer with, Austin *had* to pass to me more.

These are the things I did not like about the house with the tall fence.

I missed my friends.

Because we weren't at school and didn't know the neighborhood, we didn't get to play outside a lot.

Even though you get to kick the ball a lot more, soccer with two people isn't much fun.

After we had read every book that Mom had brought with us and explored all the places where we could make camp, I got bored. I do not like being bored.

The thing that I kind of liked and kind of did not like about the house with the tall fence was . . .

Chess.

One day Austin and I were both bored and Austin said something like, "Hey, I've got a great game we can play. It's called chess."

And I said something like, "What's that?"

He told me to go and ask Mom for some paper and scissors, and when I gave them to him, he started cutting up all these little square pieces of paper about as big as my pinkie nail. Then he got a bigger piece of paper and drew lots of lines on it. He told me to color some of the squares in, and I tried really hard to stay in the lines, but that's not easy.

When half the squares were colored in, Austin said it was ready and that we could play chess. He showed me how to place my little pieces of paper on the squares, and we took turns moving them one space forward at a time.

It was kind of interesting, kind of not interesting.

Mom came in and asked what we were doing. Austin said that we were playing chess and that he had seen two of his teachers play it before. Mom said that she thought there should be more than one kind of piece on the board.

She left and we carried on playing. I liked the way we took turns and that when it was my turn to go, I could stop and think and decide what to do. I didn't have to ask Austin to let me make my move. I could just make it.

We played for a long time, until Austin said the game was over. I didn't know if I'd won or not.

7 | PRAYER FOR A MIRACLE

OLUWATOYIN ——————

Apart from Kayode's friend who found us the house to rent, we had told nobody about our move down south. To preserve their safety, even our family did not know that we were staying nearby. It was difficult to be so close but deliberately cut ourselves off from the people we loved so much. Yet the pace of life was much slower in Akure than back in Abuja, and Kayode and I both appreciated the way the silence settled throughout the house, especially when the boys were reading or playing the combination game of chess and checkers that they had made themselves. If ever I did go out to buy rice or yams or plantains, I left Kayode at home with the boys and returned to the house quickly—not out of panic, but more because I wanted to be back with my family. When we were together like this, living quiet lives with the doors locked and the curtains drawn, it was good to savor the peace. It reminded me of the still air and silence that settles after a storm has passed.

A week after we arrived, when the boys were asleep and Kayode and I were talking quietly before bed, there was a noise from outside. It sounded like someone was shaking the fence.

Then, silence.

Kayode turned off the light and edged toward the window. I heard his breath catch in his throat.

"What is it?"

Kayode's eyes were scanning the compound from side to side. Something caught his attention, and he backed away from the window as if he had been stung by a wasp.

"Is there someone out there?"

He nodded. "Two men," he mouthed.

I looked at the front door. I knew it was locked—I had checked it four or five times already that evening—and I could see the thin metal bolt in place across the top. But part of me still wanted to go and check, to make sure the key really was turned.

"Go to the boys," whispered Kayode. "And pray. It's our only weapon. Please pray."

It was harder to leave him this time than it was before. When the men had visited five months earlier in Abuja, I had known that our house was secure and that the door was as solid as it could possibly be. This time I was leaving Kayode separated from them by just a thin door held in place by one weak bolt and a single lock. It would be only a matter of minutes before they broke through.

"Go," said Kayode. "They want me, not you or the boys. Let me try and get them away from here. You just need to pray."

And so yet again, for the second time in too few weeks, I crept into my sons' room, got down on my knees, and pleaded with God to let them sleep and to let them live.

The banging did not last long. And thanks to the thin door, I could hear far more than before. This time only one of them did the talking. I wondered if it was the same one who had waved the gun at me.

"We traced you, Adewumi. You've been escaping us for far too long, but we have you now. We know you are inside. And we know that today you will go to heaven."

The banging resumed. Back in Abuja it had been a steady bang of a fist or a shoulder to the door. A strong, steady rhythm. But not now. Now it was a frantic scramble, a wild barrage of fists and feet and shoulders raging at the thin wood.

I could hear Kayode's prayers beneath the chaos. I could hear mine too. But instead of praying that I would not become a widow, I was begging God not to let my sons become orphans.

When I heard the sound of feet scrambling inside the house, for a moment I feared the worst, that they had somehow made their way inside. But the banging on the front door was continuing, and I realized that it was Kayode running to the kitchen. There was a back door there, and I heard it crash open and then slam shut.

The men at the front must have heard it, too, for their banging suddenly fell silent. I heard the fence rattle again, even louder this time, and a new voice shout out, "Let's go! Let's go! Let's go! The police are here!"

I heard a car start in the distance and drive away, then nothing.

This time the silence did not remind me of the calm that follows a storm. It was painful. Cold. Deathly.

I thanked God for the gift of sleep, for the fact that the boys—my beautiful, deep-sleeping boys—never once stirred or showed any sign of waking. I stayed where I was for so long that my knees started to ache.

And then, when I knew I had to leave the room and find out what was on the other side of the bedroom door, I started to move. Slowly, I got to my feet and placed my hand on the door. There was no sound on the other side, but it still took me several seconds to summon the courage to open it.

The hall was empty, lit by a flashlight that we hung outside the boys' bedroom.

I checked the front door. I could see cracks in the frame, but it was still there, still locked. It was a miracle that it was still in place.

"Hello?"

Nobody replied. I took the flashlight and carried on looking around the living room. I saw Kayode's phone. His shoes. His keys.

I tried again, a little louder this time. "Hello?"

Nothing.

I crept back to check the other rooms. The bathroom was empty. Our bedroom was empty. The only room left to try was the kitchen. I wanted to leave that until last.

I opened the door to it, praying and shaking.

The shadows cast by the flashlight terrified me.

But as I searched the floor, I found some degree of comfort. I was on my knees, scanning for any sign that things had not gone the way I believed they had and that they had caught Kayode. There was no blood, no sign of any struggle. The back door was still shut. I went to lock it, then stopped myself.

Where was Kayode? What if he was outside and wanting to come in? Should I open the door and call him? What if one of the men was out there, waiting?

I inched the door open.

"Kayode," I whispered as loud as I dared. "Kayode!"

Silence.

I shut the door quickly, locked it, and tried to ram in a chair beneath the handle. I turned off the flashlight and sat down on the floor outside the boys' room. If I turned my head one way, I could see the outline of the front door. The other way I could make out the kitchen and the back door.

I did not look at either. I closed my eyes and prayed.

It is strange how loud even the smallest sound becomes when you are listening for proof of life or bracing yourself for an attack. I was alert to every noise, weighing each one in my mind. A dog barking in the distance. The breeze pushing against a gate. Even cicadas and crickets had me wondering whether they were a sign that Kayode was coming back or a clue that the Boko Haram militants were returning with reinforcements.

So I waited there in the darkness. Nothing happened around me, but everything was raging within. One moment I could be hopeful of Kayode's return while the next I would be convinced that the men had returned and were stalking in the darkness outside.

It was tempting to give in to fear, to let my thoughts drift into a waking nightmare about life as a widow or my boys making their way through life as orphans. But I knew that thinking that way would not help.

All I had was prayer.

Two hours must have passed before I finally heard a sound that I could not explain away.

A shake of the fence. The scramble of feet on the ground. The soft knock on the back door. The turning of the handle.

Trying to make no sound at all, I crept back to the kitchen.

The handle turned again.

I tried to sound brave as I called out, "Hello?"

"Oluwatoyin! It's me. Let me in!"

I pulled the chair away, threw back the locks, and opened the door enough for Kayode to scramble inside.

We hugged in the darkness. I could feel him tremble in my arms.

"Are you hurt, Kayode?"

"No. I am well. You?"

"I am fine. What happened?"

"I was praying for a miracle when they were trying to break the door down. At first I thought the door might hold them back somehow, but then I remembered the kitchen door. If they found that, then they would be in the house, and we would all be at risk. So I ran out the back and made as much noise as I could, hoping they would chase me and leave you."

He paused and put the chair back against the back door.

"I fell down on the other side of the fence and heard them say that they thought it was the police. I watched them leave, but I wanted to make sure they were not going to come back. So I've been waiting and watching. I do not think they will return tonight."

"But another night? Surely they will try again."

I could sense him stiffen. "Yes. We have to go. As soon as it is light."

8 | A NEW ESCAPE PLAN

KAYODE ——————

Right from the start of all this we were so grateful that the boys had slept through every visit from Boko Haram. We were convinced that their deep sleep was one of the main reasons they were still alive. But we knew that if they discovered the truth about the threat we were facing, fear would take over, and they would never sleep. So we made sure that they were out of the room whenever Oluwatoyin and I talked about our situation. Every time the TV news was running a story about the increasing threat of violence in the region, we turned it off.

Our boys trust us. They always have. They know that if we tell them that it's time to sleep, then they should sleep. And they know that if we tell them not to worry, then they should not worry. They trust us completely, and even though the situation with Boko Haram had grown worse with every visit, they had no fear or panic. As far as they were concerned, we were on vacation.

But even though both of them were too young to need to know, they were no fools. By the time we moved to the south, Austin was twelve years old—old enough to know when something was wrong and old enough to know when his parents were worried.

Neither Oluwatoyin nor I had been able to sleep after the men from Boko Haram visited our rented home in Akure, so even if Austin hadn't noticed the marks on the outside of the front door, our own tiredness was enough to make him suspicious.

"Are you okay, Mom?" Austin asked, as Oluwatoyin stood in the kitchen while the boys ate. She told him she was fine, just not sleeping too well in this new house.

He fell silent, studying his mom. I knew he was not convinced.

Thankfully, I had another plan. A guaranteed way of making sure that both the boys' minds were lifted fully from any present concerns and filled with joy and excitement.

"Boys," I said as they started on the dishes. "We are going to take a very special vacation. We are going to America."

This was the first time Oluwatoyin and I told them, even though we had been planning a trip for a long time. A year earlier, back when life was calm and settled and my business was thriving in Abuja, we had applied for tourist visas. Oluwatoyin had an uncle living in Dallas, and we liked the idea of taking the boys across the Atlantic for one or two months to visit their cousins and see the country that we had viewed so many times on our TV screen.

The application had taken months, but eventually our request had been granted. When our passports were returned with the stamp of approval from the US, the news spread far and wide. Friends called to congratulate us, and family members told us that we had received a great blessing.

But almost as soon as we received the visas, my work grew even busier. Months passed, the orders increased, and the machines were rarely ever silent. The idea that I might be able to take several weeks off and leave the business in someone else's hands appeared less and less likely.

And then Boko Haram showed up. By the time we packed our car and headed down to Akure, there really was no print business for me anymore. I had closed the doors soon after the very first visit. We were living off our investments, slowly waking up to the fact that the life we once knew had been torn away from us.

The US visas were an even bigger blessing than we had first thought.

9 | THOUSANDS OF MILES AND AN OCEAN AWAY

OLUWATOYIN ——————

The moment Kayode told the boys about the trip, their eyes popped and their jaws dropped.

They both whispered the word as if it were magic. "*America?* Wow. What does it look like?"

"You'll see," he said. "We will stay with your cousins in Dallas. You won't even be able to count how many times you will say 'wow' because of all the sights you will see in that country."

I love seeing Kayode when he is excited like this. His eyes grow wide, his voice booms, and his face breaks out in the biggest smile you have ever seen. It is infectious, and within an hour—once Tani had run through the top fifty of his most urgent questions—we had two boys who were so excited that they did not question why we packed up our things that very morning and drove to stay with a friend nearer to the airport.

It took two weeks before we could fly. We were busy with the task of buying tickets and gifts for our family in Dallas, and the boys were constantly chattering between themselves about the great adventure that lay ahead.

Most of the time Kayode and I were swept up with their excitement, but as we made our preparations, I could tell that the same fears that were haunting me were troubling him too.

One afternoon as we stood in our friend's house, watching our boys play with their friends in the courtyard, I stood beside him and asked the question that had been eating away at me for months. "How do you think they found us?"

I had been trying to figure it out ever since the men's first visit to our home six months earlier. I had been over it so many times, running through long lists of possible people who might have told them where we were. But while it was easy for them to find us back in Abuja, we had told only one person in Akure about our move—the friend who had found us the house. He was a Christian, a lifelong friend, and he was as close as family. There was no way that he would have betrayed us.

The only idea I could think of was the car. "Could someone have spotted us driving down here? Do you think we were followed?"

Kayode shook his head. "These people kill soldiers; they kill government ministers. They bomb churches that are protected with guards. They know how to get information and track people down. We may never know how they found us, and even if we did, what good would it do?"

We stood in silence. I wondered if Kayode was thinking the same thoughts as me: *If they found us at the first house in Akure, how long before they find us here at the second? And if they tracked us so far south, can they also track us across the ocean? Will we even be safe in America?*

I tried to shake these thoughts from my mind. I knew they would do me no good.

When I looked at Kayode, there were tears on his cheeks.

"When you know your life is in danger, it is so difficult to keep going," he said. "I know that I will not be lucky all the time. All I have to protect me is God."

I held his hand in mine. "And He will protect you and all of us, just like He has already."

Kayode looked at me. What I saw in his eyes brought tears to my own. He started to speak but struggled to find the words. Eventually, they came.

"All that matters to me is keeping you and the boys safe. I cannot do that here anymore."

I wiped my face and smiled. "Don't talk like that. America understands about keeping terrorists out. It is a safe place, a good place. As soon as we get there, we will be safe, and all of this will be thousands of miles and one large ocean away. By the time we have spent a year in Dallas, all of this will have died down. We will be able to think about returning home. And if we don't, it will be because another door has opened for us there."

Kayode smiled and nodded, but I knew his thoughts were somewhere else.

PART 2
SEARCHING
FOR HOME

10 | FAMILY CONNECTION

OLUWATOYIN ————

In some ways Kayode and I are different people who come from very different worlds. I can talk almost as much as Tani, while Kayode is more like Austin—weighing his words with thought and care before he shares them with those around him. I was raised a Muslim (although not a strict one in any sense of the word); Kayode comes from a long line of Christians. My father had almost as many wives as Muhammad, while Kayode's father married only once. I am one of twenty children; Kayode is one of just five. And while my father's ancestors were farmers, scratching out a living in the red African soil, my husband is a prince—that's right, a genuine Nigerian prince—whose grandfather served the people of the Ado Ekiti region as their *ewi*, their king.

When you are young and you fall in love, differences like these do not matter at all. Oftentimes they are part of the attraction that draws you together. Then, as you grow and raise a family, the contrasts in your background begin to take on a new significance and gain a new value. As you share with your children the stories from your youth, offer your perspective on the challenges facing them today, and listen to your husband share his own, the differences become a source of inspiration, a deep pool of experience from which you can draw.

But no matter how great the contrasts in personality and background, what matters most are the things that unite you. Your vision. Your values. Your purpose.

For Kayode and me, so much of who we are is defined by where we come from. Even though Kayode's ancestry is so much more impressive than mine and his friends really do address him as "Prince," there is one part of our history that binds us close and shapes our lives so much that we are closer than the air we breathe.

We are not just Nigerians. We are *Yoruba*.

Of the three main tribes in my homeland, Yoruba are known for being the most respectful. We talk well of people and are renowned for our willingness to help others. If you visit our territory and do happen to see someone behaving poorly in public—perhaps someone not crossing the street to help another struggling with an armful of bags or a young person not addressing an elder with the appropriate respect—you will inevitably see people begin to point and hear them call out, "Are you sure that you are Yoruba?" We take such pride in belonging to our tribe that often the question alone is enough to draw out an apology and put matters right.

Yoruba people are also famous for our hospitality. We are accommodating and generous and expect to throw our doors open to any family member who visits. We live in community with the people we love and think nothing of sharing our home and possessions with others. So, while Islam taught my father that it was permissible to take four wives and a mistress, it was the fact that he was Yoruba that led him to have all those women and children living with him under one roof.

We lived well together. So many of my childhood memories are of our compound being full to overflowing with people attending one of the many parties we held throughout the year. The air would be thick with the smell of woodsmoke, my mouth salivating at the prospect of the food on offer—jollof rice, pounded yam, soups full of spices—and at the smells that lingered for hours. When people were fed and happy, my sisters and I would get up and perform a traditional dance while several of our uncles beat out a frenzy on the drums. We'd kick and spin and smile as the crowd cheered. And with as many as one hundred adults in attendance, we'd make good money at the end as we walked among them and asked—respectfully— whether they would be willing to give us a coin or two. On nights like those, I felt as though the whole world was my home.

Kayode's family was far smaller than mine—just one father and mother and he and his four siblings—but it was even more traditional. Historically, in Yoruba families the wealthiest member builds a big home that the whole extended family can live in. Kayode's father did just that, filling his compound with a long, low building that could accommodate dozens of people. The house was built with a corridor down the middle, with several two-room apartments running off either side. In each apartment—made up of a bedroom and a parlor—was an uncle with his wife and children. The whole extended family would eat their meals together, play together, and share life together. And when Kayode's father heard of a young couple in need of accommodations because their own family lived on the other side of the country, he gave them a room to rent. Before long they, too, were thought of as family and stayed in the home for twenty years.

For Yoruba people like us, family is everything. Even though Kayode and I lived alone with our boys, we were still deeply connected to our army of aunts and uncles, cousins and siblings, grandparents and parents. Many times each year, we would all gather together, drawn like the tides toward the gravity of the moon. We belonged likewise to them, and they to us.

So it was painful to have to go into hiding when we moved to Akure and cut ourselves off from our family to keep them safe. But to leave Nigeria the way we did in June 2017 was even harder. Boko Haram had not just stolen our peace and threatened our security; it had ripped us away from our home and stolen from us our family, tearing us from the very people we had lived alongside since our first breath here on earth.

But as we flew across the Atlantic, there was one star of hope ahead of us. We were heading to Dallas, to my uncle and his American family. With so much that was unclear in the future, it was good to know that we would find a new home there.

11 | FIRST IMPRESSIONS OF AMERICA

KAYODE ————

Oluwatoyin and I were both confused. We stood in the Greyhound bus terminal in New Jersey, looking at the map.

"Fifteen hundred miles in thirty-six hours?" Oluwatoyin repeated. "Could that be a mistake?"

I knew all about long journeys. Less than a year earlier I had made a trip in Nigeria. I needed to travel to a neighboring state on business, a total distance of one hundred miles. Since most of my drive was on the freeway, I assumed that if I left early enough in the morning, I would arrive before dark. But when I reached the halfway point, the freeway had been washed away by a river. Cars and trucks swarmed in tight all around me, and soon the road was blocked solid. Like every other driver, I remained calm. These things happen in Nigeria, where the roads are often lined with potholes that cause speeding trucks and buses to flip over and lie across the road like fallen trees. In those cases, it can take twenty-four hours to get traffic moving again. But on this particular occasion, I was not just trapped for one night. I was stuck for three.

So fifteen hundred miles in thirty-six hours? Impossible.

But as soon as I climbed onto the bus, I knew things were different. The Greyhound was more luxurious than any bus I had ever ridden on at home. But it was the roads that I noticed most. As we pulled out of the city and headed west toward Pittsburgh, along freeways lined with forests and fields, not once did the bus swerve to avoid a pothole or slow to a halt and kill its engine while the road ahead was cleared. We just drove, strong and steady, farther and farther away from Nigeria.

After thirteen sleepless hours of flying and almost half that long waiting in line at airports, thirty-six hours on a bus gives you a lot of time to yourself. And while the boys and Oluwatoyin were able to sleep for some of the journey to Dallas, I was awake and thinking.

I did not mind so much. With every hour that passed and every mile we sped along, I felt happier.

For the first time in months, I let my thoughts drift. I was able to put most of my worries about Boko Haram from my mind. I allowed myself to think about this new adventure we were beginning.

Of course, I had been thinking a lot about America ever since we decided to take the vacation, but now that we were finally here, my thoughts took on new shapes. As we drove past car dealerships the size of farms and billboards that rose into the air like ships' sails, I recognized it all. Even though I had never seen an environment so consistently wealthy before, it was still so familiar to me.

How can one country be so good at planting its image in the minds of people who live thousands of miles away? I remembered the way people responded to the news of our visas, how old friends and relatives from far and wide called to pass on their congratulations, as if we had not been granted visas but won some national honor or been awarded a life-changing cash prize. None of them had ever been to America, and I doubted whether any of them would ever be fortunate enough to visit, but they all knew that the opportunity ahead of us was truly great.

Yet some of them were wrong in how easy they imagined it to be. I remember one friend telling me, "As soon as you arrive in the New York, you will see dollars lying in the road. You can pick them up and become rich just like that!" I never believed him, but I shared his joy and optimism. And by the time I was sitting on the bus, next to my sleeping wife and behind my two sleeping boys, I knew that if something good was going to happen in my life, it was bound to happen here in America.

We stopped every few hours. Cleveland. Indianapolis. Saint Louis. Tulsa. Some places I had heard of; other names were new to me. But at every stop there were bright lights and vending machines and clean water in the bathrooms and people smiling at us. Everything worked. Nothing was broken. And every time we climbed back on board the bus again, my confidence in America grew just a little bit stronger.

By the time we stepped off the bus and stood stretching and yawning in the Dallas evening, watching Oluwatoyin's uncle and his wife waving to us from inside the terminal, I was convinced that we had arrived in the greatest place on the planet.

12 | WHERE THE LIGHTS DON'T GO OUT

TANI ————

In Nigeria the lights are *always* going out. You can be watching TV or be on your computer and then *bang*! Just like that, there's no more electricity in your house.

When I was a really little kid, I used to think that it was because we had to take turns to share the electricity with the other houses. But then I realized that the whole city would be without lights for lots of days, so it wasn't about sharing. One day I asked my dad about the lights, and he said that it is because of people who are corrupt and act like thieves, but I never really got how you can steal something you can't see.

Most of the time when the lights went out in my home, it was okay, though. All I had to do was ask Mom or Dad or Austin to go outside and start the generator, and then the lights would come back on.

But if you don't have a generator, it's not so good.

So when we got to Dallas and arrived at the new house where my cousins lived, and they fed us spaghetti and fish and rice, and Mom and Dad laughed and smiled and looked really, really happy, I looked for the generator. I couldn't find one. I was thinking that maybe the house wasn't so good after all. I wanted to ask the woman that Mom told us all to call Grandma (even though she wasn't our *real* grandma), "What do you do when the lights go out?" But she was kinda scary, and so I kept quiet.

But then I realized something. We'd been in America for almost three days already, and the lights hadn't gone out.

I had never counted the days at home, but I knew that the lights could be out for a long, long time. Like days and days and weeks and weeks. It gets so common that it's actually weird when you *don't* hear the sound of generators running.

I was counting the days, and when I got to ten, I knew I had to tell Mom about it. "We've been here ten days now, and the lights have not gone off even *once!*"

She smiled and her eyes went all big, the way they did whenever I told her that I'd done well at school or that I loved her. And I knew that she was amazed just like I was.

13 | ADAPTING TO CULTURAL DIFFERENCES

OLUWATOYIN ——————

At first everything in Dallas was good. Growing up in a house with nineteen siblings and four stepmoms, I learned from a young age to love a crowd. I am comfortable living in small spaces with others, when every movement around the home is like a dance as you weave and swirl around each other. So the fact that my uncle and his wife shared their house with some of their adult children and several teenage grandchildren made me happy. It was good to be back in the chaos and warmth of a large family.

It was even better to be with my uncle. Even though I'd spoken to him regularly on the phone over the years, I'd never actually met him in person before. My mom and he had talked all the time on the phone when I was growing up, and I always enjoyed joining in on the calls. Meeting him in person was wonderful. He was so gentle and kind and reminded me so much of my mom, his sister, that I immediately felt at home in his presence.

However, some things were a little more different than I expected.

My uncle had immigrated to America forty years earlier, and he was not married to a Nigerian. His wife—whom we instinctively called Grandma out of respect—was an African-American woman, and she could not have been more different from him. He was quiet, laid-back, and preferred to let life take its course rather than stress about things. His wife was full of energy and passion, and it was obvious that she was the kind of woman who was comfortable making decisions and directing the group. So when it was time to go with the family to church on the first Sunday that we were there, it was Grandma who stood by the front door and shouted at the whole house until we were all ready to leave. She was the one who drove, the one who chose our seats, and the one who decided where we would eat after the service.

Kayode and I knew there would be many cultural differences between Nigeria and America, so we chose not to let any of this trouble us. In fact, I knew that my uncle had been having some health problems, and he looked thinner than he did in the pictures he had sent us. So part of me was grateful that he had married a woman who would relieve him of any unnecessary burdens.

But I would be lying if I said that everything was perfect.

When we were first shown into the house and introduced to my uncle's grandchildren, I did what any Nigerian woman would do and opened my arms wide for a hug and let the joyous smile that was burning within me shine on my face. To meet close family like this for the first time was a wonderful thing, and I was so excited to get to know them.

"Hi!" I sang and walked over to Damian, the youngest. He was thirteen years old and sitting on the couch and playing a video game. "Give me a hug, Damian! We're family!"

He didn't take his eyes off the screen. But he did speak. "Do I have to?"

I froze, my arms still held wide like the wings of a hovering bird.

It was awkward.

I turned back to Grandma, but she just shrugged and sank down into her couch.

Kayode and I were given a room to ourselves, while Tani and Austin were given beds in the same room as Damian and his older brother, Terrell. At first everything was good. But within a few days, there were arguments breaking out between the boys. It was nothing unusual, nothing unexpected even. Just Terrell or Damian complaining about their stuff being touched or moved. But it bothered our boys. They had never before encountered someone who was a blood relative who did not treat them as such.

"Family can never be smooth all the time," I told them many times. "All we can do is act in a loving way and try to get along."

My uncle could see what was going on, and he had a suggestion of his own. He told us that it was like this every time his grandkids were on vacation. "They sit down in front of that TV and play their games all day long. It's only a matter of time before they start getting on each other like this. But they'll be back at school next week. Why don't you enroll Austin and Tani too?"

Kayode and I both liked the idea immediately. My own father had valued education above all things, and between the school closures in Abuja and our brief vacation in Akure, the boys had missed more school than we were happy with. So, with Grandma's help, I took the passports, immunization cards, and two not-so-happy Adewumi boys to the local school and signed them up to start the following week.

With them at school, surely we would finally be able to settle. Wouldn't we?

14 | RESTLESS WITHOUT WORK

KAYODE ———————

My father was the son of a king, but he still had to work. By the time I was born, my father had established his own construction business. By the time I was old enough to hold a shovel, he was ready to put me to work. I helped where I could, digging and carrying and fetching at home.

When I was ten years old, my father won a contract to build a hotel outside the city. Each Saturday he would take my brother and me to the building site. We were children, but there was no playing for us. Instead, we were each given a job to do. We fetched water and wood, mixed mortar, and cleaned the tools at the end of the day. It was hot, hard work, and there were times when I complained, "Why are you making us work like this?"

My father would look at me, place his hands on his hips, and lock his eyes on mine. "I am teaching you how to make it in life. You are a prince, but do you want to be a king like my father? Nobody will ever choose a lazy person to be king. Never rely on your family name alone. Work hard, always."

I knew he was right. In our region kings are a little like governors, senators, or mayors and are chosen by a group of ten or fifteen people who are the kingmakers. Anyone who wants to be king must be of good character and well-known in society. All the same, I listened to my father's lectures, not really appreciating the wisdom in his words but looking forward to the moment when I lined up at the end of each day and received my wages. And when I had saved enough money to buy my first radio, the lesson had finally been learned.

Years later when I owned my printshop, I decided to walk in my father's footsteps. I worked hard at any and every task that was before me. Whether it was finding customers and negotiating contracts or carrying paper around the shop and bringing my machine operators the tools or equipment they needed, I was always willing to work.

So laziness has never been an option for me.

When we arrived in Dallas, Oluwatoyin and I both wanted to work. My wife dedicated herself to sweeping and mopping the floors every morning, to preparing food and keeping the whole house tidy. But me? Our uncle and Grandma owned an airport shuttle business, and I asked him if I could help in any way, perhaps by driving some of the shifts.

He said no. "This is America. You cannot work unless you have your papers. So it is best that you forget about this idea of having a job. Relax, enjoy yourself, take a break. Sit at home. It's better than working."

I did not like any of those words. How could sitting around the house all day be better than working?

By the time the boys started at school, I was feeling restless. Within a week or two, I had grown frustrated. Days went by, and all I did was sleep, eat, take walks around the block, and lie on the bed waiting for something to happen. It never did.

"Uncle," I asked one morning when he was about to head out the door and start work. "Please, is there nothing I can do? I need to work."

"No," he said, looking nervous. "You probably shouldn't even be walking around outside so much, at least not without your passport. This is America, and they can deport you just like that if you break the rules."

He closed the front door behind him. I listened to the car start and wanted to call out that I was not breaking any rules. I wanted to tell him that I did not see work as a crime and that I thought America would recognize that hard work was a good thing.

I said nothing, though.

Instead, I walked back to the bedroom and lay down on the bed.

I had gone from being a prisoner of my own fear in Nigeria to becoming a prisoner of my uncle's fear in America.

It was no way for a man to live.

15 | TEARS ALL AROUND

TANI ——————

At first things were good in Dallas, even though we had to go to school. I liked the way the library was full of books and there were so many computers that nobody had to share. I liked it when Damian was playing his video games and he didn't notice me watching from the doorway. And I liked the way that in Dallas you could go out to a restaurant and eat food from any country in the world.

But then two things happened, and life in Dallas got bad. Not just kind of bad. Really bad.

The first thing was something with my dad. After I had been at school for two or three weeks, he told me that he was going back to Nigeria. I asked him something like, "Why are you going back already? We only just got here."

He said, "I need to go back so that I can sell my machines and come back with enough money to live here."

I did not like it. I don't think Mom liked it either, because after he left, she started looking really worried and sad. Sometimes when I walked into her room, she tried to pretend that she had not just been crying.

The other problem was the boys. Mom and Dad had told Austin and me to be really friendly to them. It worked for Austin, but it did not work for me. Even though I tried to ask lots of questions, they wouldn't talk to me. They'd stare at me like I was dirty. They'd kick my stuff around the bedroom. And then they started getting in my face about things.

There was one time when I was licking my finger because we had eaten candy and some of it had gotten stuck on my fingernail.

Terrell walked up to me and hit me on the head. He said, "Don't lick your finger around me, kid."

Mom saw. She was angry. "Why did you have to do that? We're family!"

Terrell said, "We're not family!" Then Uncle came in, and the two of them started fighting together. Well, it wasn't really that they were fighting together. Terrell was shouting and shouting and saying things that I didn't believe a kid would *ever* say to an adult. But he just kept shouting, and Uncle just stood there like he didn't mind being shouted at. I was waiting for Uncle to make Terrell stop, but he didn't. He just stood and listened while Terrell was yelling so hard that there were these little bubbles of spit flying out of his mouth.

It was surprising. I'd never seen a kid talk to an adult that way. I guess Mom didn't want me to see too much because she told me to go to her bedroom and read a book.

Later that night Mom and I were both crying.

16 | WORN-OUT WELCOME

OLUWATOYIN ————

"We are safe here," I said, when Kayode first spoke of returning alone to Nigeria. "Why go back?"

"You are right," he said. "We are safe. We can sleep with two eyes closed in Dallas. There is no Boko Haram to trouble us. But being safe is not the same as being fully alive. We have no power here. There is no chance of working, and all I am doing is sleeping, eating, and waiting for bed. I cannot live this life."

I knew that I could not argue with him, and I knew that he was right, so I did not try.

"I need to work," he said. "That is why I must return. Let me sell the machines and the property. Then when I return, we will have money to hire a lawyer who can help us get work permits."

"But it is not safe there."

"I will stay with my brother. I will only go out at night. And I will not go anywhere near the shop. I promise, Oluwatoyin, I will manage myself and be careful. And this is the only way. If we want to try and make a home here, I have to return and sell everything. It is the only way."

I did not like it, but I agreed with him. My uncle took a different view. He told him that he should not travel back, that leaving the country was a mistake. "Stay here and rest," he said.

Kayode looked at my uncle. "Rest?" The word was like a cancer to him.

One month after we arrived in America, Kayode returned to Nigeria. Within a few days of me standing at the bus station in Dallas, wiping tears from my face as I waved goodbye, things changed in the house.

The first sign was easy to ignore. One of my uncle's granddaughters stopped calling me Aunty and started calling me by my name. Not a big deal, but I never heard her address my uncle or his wife by their names. The way she said it, and the way she stared at me defiantly, I knew that it was deliberate and that it was meant as a sign of disrespect.

I was unable to sleep at night, so I put it down to me being tired and stressed and to my uncle's grandkids not being used to sharing their home with people. I told myself that it was nothing to bother about and that she was just being a kid.

Sunday came around, and I made sure that the boys and I were smartly dressed and ready to go to church as usual. When it was time to go and I heard Grandma and Uncle at the front door, I hurried out and warmly greeted her.

"How are you, Grandma? Did you sleep well? Can I help you with your bags?"

She did not look at me.

I thought maybe she was tired like I was, so I carried on. "I like the dress you are wearing. I've not seen that before."

Nothing.

"Are we going to church now, Grandma? Shall I call the boys out?"

It was as if I were a ghost.

She walked back into the kitchen, leaving me standing there, confused. I stared at my uncle, hoping for an explanation.

"I'm sorry," he said. "I did not tell you earlier that you will not be able to go to church with Grandma."

"Is she unwell?"

"What? Oh, yes. She just needs to rest. You should too."

My response was to get up earlier in the morning, find even more cleaning tasks to take on, and make sure that whenever I saw Grandma in the morning, I was even more polite and respectful than usual.

Most of the time she would flash me a half smile, tell me that she was fine, and hurry on through to whichever room I was not in. But two or three days after the church incident, she finally spoke to me.

"When is he coming back?"

I had just returned from walking the boys to school and was confused by her question. Did she mean Tani or Austin?

"Your husband. When is he coming back? When do you plan on moving out?"

The words were piling up in my head like storm clouds. In the week before Kayode left, we had tried to sit down with her and my uncle to explain our plan for Kayode to return within a month or so, for the two of us to find work, and then for the four of us to move out within a few more months. But Grandma had told us that she was too busy to talk, and my uncle told us not to worry.

Standing in the living room, missing Kayode more than ever, I tried to explain the plan to Grandma. But before I even finished my first sentence, she lost interest. She turned on the TV and shook her head.

I crept out of the room.

Later I told my uncle. He said I should not worry about any of it. Having grown up in Nigeria, my belief is that when someone like an uncle or a parent tells you not to worry, there really is no point in worrying. Their job is to protect you; their job is to make sure all is well. Your job is to trust them and do what they say.

But I worried all the same.

After that, things worsened.

I started trying to avoid Grandma as much as possible. If she was in the house when the boys were at school, I would stay in the bedroom. Only when I'd heard the front door open would I peer through the window to see her leave. Then I would let myself out.

Food became an issue as well. The milk and various other supplies that I'd bought and shared with everyone were suddenly relocated to a separate shelf in the fridge. When her grandkids were hungry and shouting for her to make them a snack, I'd offer them some of the rice I'd made, but they'd refuse. Bit by bit, any sign that we were family was wiped away.

I did not like it at all, and I started to wonder if it was my fault. In the hours I would spend each day lying on the bed, waiting for Grandma to leave, I went over the same two questions. *Am I the one causing all this? Was it a mistake to come to Dallas?* I never found an answer.

I tried to keep my troubles away from my uncle. He hadn't been looking well when we arrived, and as we entered the second week of Kayode's trip, he started to look worse. He was taking his own advice and resting as much as possible, but it did not appear to be helping.

For me, some days were harder than others. If the boys were finding it tough, and Tani had been crying because of something Damian or Terrell said or did, I'd feel worse. The guilt would be heavier, and the feeling of being trapped would be stronger.

Kayode and I spoke on the phone when we could. He was worried about us all, but we both knew that the best thing he could do to help us in Dallas was dedicate himself to selling everything and returning to us as soon as possible. So most of the time I did not talk about things like the fridge or the grandkids being disrespectful or Grandma being rude. I wanted to hear about him, to know that he was keeping safe and that he was happy with the way the sales were all progressing.

But one day it all felt like too much.

When Kayode and I spoke on the phone, within moments he sounded concerned. I knew he could hear the stress in my voice. "What is wrong?" he asked.

The words came at the same time as the tears. "If you are loved, even if you are drinking only water, you will be fine," I answered. "But to be somewhere without love, you cannot be happy. It is tough here. It is hard. There is no love. They are getting tired of us."

17 | SORRY GOES A LONG WAY

TANI —————————

Our cousins in Dallas liked Austin more than they liked me. If he was in the living room when they were in there, they didn't mind so much. They even let him play video games with them. But if I even walked past them and touched them by accident, they'd start yelling that I wasn't allowed out of the bedroom and should go back there *right now*.

It wasn't just me that they shouted at. They shouted at each other *a lot*. Sometimes they even shouted at Mom, even though she never did anything wrong.

I was confused about it all. It didn't make sense that young people talked to adults like this, or that family didn't feel like family.

One night when I was going to bed, I said to Mom that I didn't understand what was going on.

She smiled at me and said, "It's fine. Families are different, that's all. But we love each other, right?"

I thought for a moment. Mom always tells us "sorry goes a long way" and "let sorry be always in your mouth." So I asked, "But do they say sorry to you for getting mad at you when you haven't even done anything?"

Mom shook her head. She waited awhile, like she was trying to find the right words. "But we can still forgive, can't we?"

I wanted to say no and then go to sleep, but I knew she was right. Mom's always right about that kind of thing.

18 | FROM BAD TO WORSE

OLUWATOYIN ————————

Things in my uncle's house continued to worsen. But it wasn't just the fact that Grandma could erupt at any time and accuse me or the boys of anything from stealing her things to upsetting her children and grandchildren. What made life particularly difficult was the fact that she could also be nice. She could be polite, warm, and hospitable, just like she had been when we first arrived. But then, without warning, her mood could turn. You never knew what you were going to get.

Ever since Kayode had returned to Nigeria, Grandma's moods had been getting more and more extreme. I tried being even more polite and respectful, and I tried waking up even earlier and cleaning even more of the house, but nothing worked. Grandma still flicked between moods as if there were a faulty switch somewhere inside her.

The only thing I found that worked was keeping quiet and avoiding her as much as possible. If she couldn't see me or the boys, I hoped that Grandma's anger would find a different target.

Not long after Kayode returned home, I met a woman from Nigeria named Remi. She worked with one of Grandma's daughters at a local hospital, and I had been talking on the phone to her about settling down in America. She was the first person who ever told me about claiming asylum and getting work permits and green cards. Thanks to her advice, we were able to take our first steps and begin applying.

From time to time Remi would offer to come and visit me at the house so we could talk more freely, but I always tried to avoid it. Something told me that if she came to the house, Grandma would not be happy about it.

Just a few days after the boys and I had been accused of stealing from Grandma—when Kayode had been gone for a month—Remi called one evening when I was about to tell Tani to get ready for bed.

She sounded bright and happy, just like she always did. "I'm in the neighborhood, and I'm coming over. I've got apple juice and cookies. I know where the house is, so I'll see you in ten, okay? Bye!"

I panicked. Before I could find my voice, Remi had ended the call.

I found my uncle in the front yard and told him that a friend was about to come over. He looked almost as anxious as I felt. "You've got to tell her," he said, nodding toward the living room. I knew exactly who he meant.

"Excuse me, Grandma," I said quietly as I stood inside the doorway. "I have a friend who wants to visit and say hi this evening. Would that be okay with you?"

"Sure," she said, barely lifting her eyes from the TV but waving her hand and half smiling. "No problem, no problem. That's okay."

I didn't want Remi knocking on the door and disturbing Grandma, so I waited outside in silence with my uncle. We were both nervous. I think we both feared what was coming.

In the end, it was fine. Remi arrived, and we all walked into the living room, where she told Uncle and me about how she had been able to get her citizenship. It was helpful, and Grandma even got up and came to say hi. We drank some of the juice, ate some of the cookies, and then, fifteen minutes after she arrived, Remi left.

The next morning, at 6:22 a.m., my phone buzzed. It was a text message from Grandma.

"Don't you ever invite another woman to my house. That's disrespectful. If you disrespect me again, you're out."

Even though my uncle had left Nigeria when I was a baby, and I had never met him face-to-face until we arrived in Dallas, I loved him greatly. He and my mother had been close, and she would talk about him all the time when I was young. She'd tell us how he was a kind, gentle man, how he did not like conflict and did not get angry. He was a man of peace, and the pleasure I took from living in his house was often enough to outweigh the sadness and frustration caused by his wife and grandchildren.

But the longer we stayed in Dallas, the more aware I became of how little I really knew my uncle. For example, I knew that he had been ill before we arrived—when we were back in Nigeria, he had told me about having surgery on his stomach—but it was not until I saw him with his shirt off one morning that I realized how many times he had been operated on. His belly had five or six different scars on it, some as long as my finger. He laughed when he saw me looking and changed the subject when I tried to get him to tell me what exactly was wrong with him.

I knew nothing about how Uncle and Grandma had met, nothing about what life had been like for him in America. Whenever I asked him, he gave me vague answers and not much more. I tried to get him to talk by showing him photographs from old family albums, but he only glanced at them, smiled vaguely, and moved on. It was strange, but Grandma was a lot more curious about these photos than he was. More than once she and I spent twenty or thirty minutes sitting side by side in the living room, swiping in silence through the photos I had saved on my phone.

His past and his scars were mysteries. However, he could not hide everything from me.

One afternoon I returned from walking Tani and Austin home from school to see him standing outside in the front yard, speaking on the phone. It was November and cold, but he was wearing just a thin undershirt and pants that looked as though they had been torn by a dog.

The closer I got, the worse he looked. His pants weren't just torn; they were stained with blood as well. And his arms were cut and bleeding where patches of skin had been scraped off. His shirt was lying on the ground.

He didn't look up as we approached. He was too busy talking on the phone.

I stood close to him and waited for him to finish his call. "What happened?" I asked when his trembling hands had finally been able to put the cell phone in his pocket.

He looked at me as though he were surprised to find me there. "Oh," he said, smiling and brushing some dirt from his trousers. "I fell out of a tree."

I'd almost forgotten that the boys were with me when Tani held out a hand and pointed at the road. "Which tree did you fall out of, Uncle? Was it that big one there? Or the tall, skinny one by the garage?" Uncle shook his head, but Tani continued, listing all the trees he could think of in the neighborhood. "If you tell me, then I will know which one, and I'll be careful not to climb it myself."

Austin took Tani inside, and I was left staring.

My uncle bent down to pick up his shirt but fumbled it, so I helped him put it back on. It seemed to me that he must have aged ten years in ten days.

"What happened?" I asked again.

"She . . ." he said, his voice trailing off as he looked back at the house then up and down the road. He took a step toward me and lowered his voice. "We had a fight."

I wanted to ask all the questions that were shouting in my head, but I knew I needed to keep quiet and let him tell me in his own time.

"We were in the house, arguing. She was mad and said she needed to get away. I didn't want her to drive angry, so I followed her out to the driveway. I opened the passenger door and was trying to persuade her to get out of the car and come back inside and talk some more, but she just ignored me. She started reversing back down the driveway. But the door was still open, and it caught me and pulled me with it. I got dragged all the way to the road."

"Didn't she stop? Did she help you at all?"

He shook his head. "No. But, listen. It was an accident. I don't think she saw me at all."

"Where did she go?"

"I don't know. But I know she'll be back."

We both stood in silence for a while. Eventually, I couldn't hold the question in any longer. "Uncle, what were you fighting about?"

This time he didn't look back to the house or along the street. He just looked right at me, his old, sad eyes full of defeat and pain. He didn't say anything. He didn't need to.

"Was it us? Was that what you were arguing about?"

He shook his head, but we both knew he was lying.

I smiled and gave him a hug. "It's okay, Uncle."

He smiled a little, then shuffled inside. I walked behind him. By the time we reached the kitchen, I had decided something. I did not want their marriage to suffer because of us, so the next time I spoke with Kayode on the phone, I would have to tell him that we needed to leave.

19 | MOVING AGAIN

It took less than thirty seconds for my life to be transformed by Oluwatoyin. I was twenty-six years old, standing with a friend in the market in my home city of Ado Ekiti, showing him the car I had recently purchased. It was a two-year-old Toyota Camry that gleamed brilliant white in the midday sun, and my friend was impressed.

My eyes were elsewhere.

I was looking at the beautiful young woman who was walking in the market with her sisters. The way she floated from one stall to another. The easy laugh that ignited so many smiles on the faces of the passersby. And those eyes! I was under her spell in an instant.

"Prince," said my friend from inside my car. "Prince! What is it?"

"Look," I said. "Do you see that girl with the head scarf over there?"

"Yes . . . oh, wow!"

I knew right then, at that very moment, that she was the greatest woman on the face of the earth. So when I next spoke, not a single note of doubt was in my voice. "I am going to marry her."

With that, I walked over to her. I threw my chest out and held my head high, all a bluff to hide the nerves inside.

I greeted her with a smile. She was even more beautiful up close than she was from a distance. For a second my words stuck in my throat.

She returned my smile, and I found my voice. I looked her in the eye and let my words fill the air. "A day will come when you will be my wife."

She laughed.

But it was not a cold laugh or one that sent me away. It was warm, as if the idea filled her with as much joy as it did me.

That was in July. We started spending time together, and soon she took me home to meet her father. The fact that he was a Muslim and I was a Christian did not cause any conflict. In fact, it hardly came up. He asked about my job, and I told him I was a printer. He explained that he was an accountant at one of the biggest presses in the town, and we became immediate friends.

Before too long I proposed to Oluwatoyin, and almost one year after I first saw her in the market in Ado Ekiti, she became my wife. Our wedding celebration was more like a carnival. It lasted three days, and more than fifteen hundred people attended. My life had never felt so blessed.

Leaving Oluwatoyin and the boys to return to Nigeria was not easy, and I was anxious to get back to them as soon as possible. When I finally did make the long journey back to America, the welcome at the bus station in Dallas was not like the first welcome we all received when we arrived in June. It was dark, and the wind was cold, and there was no Grandma smiling and waving. There was no Uncle either. There were just my wife and my two boys.

I did not mind. They were the only people I needed.

But the joy of being reunited with my family and the relief at having successfully completed my task was short-lived. Oluwatoyin had already prepared me by telling me there was trouble at home. By the time we went to bed that night and Oluwatoyin had finished telling me in her quietest voice about the changes that had taken place, I had no misunderstanding about how bad things had become.

She told me all about what happened when Grandma had driven away and caught Uncle in the car door, how Grandma went missing for five days, and how she had returned just two days before I did. As soon as she had walked back into the house, she told Oluwatoyin the new rules that she had decided to introduce:

- The boys were no longer allowed in the living room.
- If they were not in their bedroom, they could only be in the kitchen or the bathroom.
- If Oluwatoyin or I were to go for a walk in the evening or on the weekend, we could not leave the boys at home. They would have to come with us.
- No visitors.
- No touching any food in the refrigerator that we did not buy ourselves.

The rules left me feeling confused. But the knowledge that, even though Oluwatoyin had done everything possible to protect him, Tani had been teased and bullied by the grandchildren made me angry. Even in the few hours I had been around them since I got back, I could tell that our boys were troubled by life at home. They understood what was going on, and they knew that their cousins, aunts, and grandma were rejecting them.

I tried to encourage them, telling them now that I had concluded my business in Nigeria, we would soon be able to move on with our lives. "We will get our own place, and everything will be fine."

"When?" asked Tani.

"These things take time in America. We need to be able to work first. But soon, I promise. Just a few more months."

It did not take long for me to realize that we did not have months of grace left in the house. Within minutes of seeing Grandma again for the first time, I knew that we had to go much, much sooner. I tried telling her about the success of my trip and how we now had enough money to hire a lawyer who could represent us and help us secure the proper authorization to find work and then get an apartment of our own. My words were worthless. She brushed them aside with her hand and left.

I had to steady myself before I went back into the bedroom to tell Oluwatoyin. When I finished talking, she looked just as shocked as I felt.

When you offer an invitation to family members to come stay with you in Nigeria, you assume that they will remain for some time. Not days, weeks, or even months. When you open your home to family, you expect that they will be with you for years. Perhaps even forever. The only thing that is not unclear is the fact that the invitation has no expiration date. Family is family, blood is blood, and home is home.

As a child, I grew up surrounded by family members, cousins and aunts and uncles, as well as the couple who rented a room and were soon adopted into our family. My dad would never allow any of his children to say, "This is *my* house." We shared whatever we had, and that was all that was to be said on the matter. In more than forty years of living in Nigeria, neither I nor Oluwatoyin had ever heard of anyone asking anyone who was family to leave.

Even though we knew that we should expect things in America to be different from Nigeria, it still hurt. In a way it was a deeper cut than being chased by Boko Haram. At least we expected the militant Islamists to hate us, to want to drive us from their land, or even to kill us. But family? This feeling that I had of being rejected by someone who was supposed to love and care for us was a deep wound. And it was a wound that seemed to me as though it had grown too deep to heal.

We tried talking to Uncle, and he said he would try and fix everything for us, but we knew that he was unlikely to succeed. Grandma was not Yoruba, not even Nigerian. How could we expect her to behave like one?

And so I dedicated myself to a new task of finding a home as quickly as I possibly could. At first I looked in Dallas. I hoped that I could find a small place to live and a low-paying job and move out. It was no use. With no employer, no citizenship, and nothing more than the $5,000 I had brought back from Nigeria (a sum that I soon came to realize was not nearly as impressive in America as it was back home), I was told again and again that there was nothing anyone could do to help. Every door I tried remained firmly locked.

I pressed on. I contacted every person I could think of who lived in America. I approached friends I had not had contact with for years, telling them about our situation and begging them for help.

With each hour that passed and each message I received informing me that there was nothing anyone could do, the pressure increased. The greater the pressure, the more and more desperate I felt. It was as if we were facing an executioner, and he was already loading the bullets into his gun.

There was one choice still open to us. We could return to Nigeria.

Even though my own trip back had been uneventful, I never once considered abandoning America and taking the family back. In many ways, we had even less freedom living under Grandma's roof than we did under our own in Abuja. We had surrendered our independence twice, and neither of us liked it. Both Oluwatoyin and I agreed that by far the most important thing was the boys' future. We wanted them to grow up somewhere they would be safe, where they would be able to thrive, where they would be able to work hard and enjoy the rewards. We would do whatever it took to make that happen. No matter how low we would have to stoop or how hard we would have to work, we agreed that we had been blessed to make it to America, and there was no way we were going to voluntarily walk away from it.

I had given Grandma a deadline of when we would leave, but it approached with alarming speed. With three days remaining I was searching on Facebook for any contacts I might have overlooked. I found someone I was in high school with who was now living in Atlanta. I told him the same story I had told everyone—how we had been forced to leave Nigeria, and now, after five months of living in Dallas, we urgently needed a place to live and a job.

"Yes," he replied. "You may come and stay with me for a month. I can find you work. But I do not have room for your family. Leave them in Dallas until you are ready to move into a place of your own."

It was a kind gesture, and I appreciated his offer, but leaving Oluwatoyin and the boys at Grandma's house was not an option. So I declined, thanked him greatly, and went back to scrolling through endless pages of friends of friends, desperately hoping that I might see someone I had overlooked.

With two days to go, I did. Olufemi was a school friend of mine from senior year, now living in New York.

I sent a friend request, hoping he would respond quickly.

Within the hour he had accepted, and I messaged him with my urgent request: "Please, can you help me? I am living in Dallas but have to leave by the weekend . . ."

I added some more details, pressed send, and prayed.

His reply was swift and clear.

"Our home is not big, but you are welcome to come with your whole family. And I would like to introduce you to my pastor, Pastor Phillip. He will help you."

One week after I arrived back in Dallas, we were ready to head back to the bus station again. Grandma was tired that morning, too tired to do anything more than come to her bedroom door, quickly say goodbye, and disappear again.

Uncle drove us, and before we had backed into the street from the driveway, he was already apologizing.

"You know what we men are like," he said. "We're so proud and don't like to admit when we're wrong. But I'm so sorry about all this. I'm sorry that I couldn't keep everyone happy. Sorry that I couldn't keep you here. And Grandma's sorry about this too; she really is."

"Uncle," I said. "We appreciate your words and your love for us, but you do not have to feel bad. We have never questioned your kindness or love, and we are grateful for your mighty gift of allowing us to stay in your home for five months."

It was quiet in the car, and I weighed my next words carefully.

"We were strangers to you, yet you embraced us and gave us a home. We know that it has not been easy. We understand."

"I'll take care of it," Uncle added as we pulled into the bus station. "I'll take care of it. I'll take care of everything."

I did not know quite what he meant by that or how to respond to his words. Oluwatoyin embraced him for a long time.

Eventually, when it was time to board the bus, we said goodbye.

The road north was familiar now. I recognized the farms and forests, and I no longer sat and stared, amazed at how ordered the environment was or how smooth the roads were. Instead, I barely looked outside the window as we drove. I was lost in my own thoughts, caught between two different feelings.

I was frustrated that I had wasted almost five months in America. In all that time I had not been able to do a single day's work. I had built no foundation for my family and made no progress toward a better, stronger life.

But that was not all, I had to remind myself. We were safe. We were free, and we were heading to New York. I leaned over to Oluwatoyin and whispered the words that were growing louder and louder inside me.

"Now life really starts."

PART 3
HOPE
RESTORED

20 | NEW LIFE IN NEW YORK

OLUWATOYIN ———————

I spent much of the time on the bus thinking. Thinking about what went wrong in Dallas. Thinking about my uncle and the scars on his stomach and the cuts on his arms and legs. Thinking about what other wounds we had inflicted on him and his marriage during our time in his house. What would happen to him next? Would the fighting continue? Would everything return to normal now that we had gone?

I tried to find a reason why things did not work out. I remembered how well we would speak to each other over the phone before my family left Nigeria, and how Grandma had always sounded so warm and friendly on those calls. And at the start of our time in Dallas, her welcome had been just as warm and kind as we could have hoped for. She had taken us to church, to restaurants, even helped enroll the boys in school—so she must have known that we were going to stay for a long time. But something had changed when Kayode returned to Nigeria. Was that the cause of her shift in attitude? Or was it something to do with my uncle?

I had no answer for these questions, of course, but I asked them all the same.

Most of all, I spent the bus journey thinking about something my uncle had said the day we told him about our plans to leave for New York. He'd called it a *Hail Mary*, and I'd had to ask him to repeat the words and then to explain what they meant.

As we moved north through the night, passing state line after state line, measuring our journey in the hour-long stops we made in brightly lit bus terminals along the way, my uncle's words came back to me again and again. *A Hail Mary*. Yes, I thought, that was exactly what we were doing. Heading to a city we had never been to before, a city where there was no family to greet us, to welcome us, to protect and house us. A city where terrorists had already brought fear and death. A city where our money would run out even quicker than it would in Dallas. We were heading to a city we knew nothing about and trusting that somehow things would work out. Hoping that God would go before us. Believing that no matter how rejected and defeated we felt leaving our family in Dallas, better things were ahead for us.

When we finally reached Olufemi's house in Queens, two things were immediately obvious. First was the fact that he had been honest with Kayode about his house not being suitable for us all to stay in. The house was half the size of Uncle's house and had just two bedrooms. He and his wife had five children, most of them younger than Tani.

The other thing I noticed was that Olufemi and his wife were 100 percent Yoruba. They welcomed us with such warmth and love that we instantly forgot about our tired bodies. Olufemi's wife cooked a true Nigerian feast, and within minutes we had settled. I joined her in the kitchen, closing my eyes and inhaling the familiar smells of spices that filled the air. The boys played with the little ones, and Kayode and Olufemi talked at length about life in New York.

That night, just before we laid out the mattresses in the sitting room and prepared for sleep, Olufemi gave Kayode some clear advice.

"You are in America now. You have to forget that you were the CEO back in Nigeria. You have to put aside the part of you that was the chairman of your company. Here you just have to do whatever you can."

I watched Kayode absorb the news. My husband had built a successful business in Abuja, and had we stayed in Akure, I know it would not have been long before he would have built another one. He is resourceful and reliable and knows when to take a risk and when to walk away from one. He is a born CEO, a natural chairman, a businessman to his bones. People back home looked to him for advice and trusted his opinion. And here was Olufemi telling him to leave all that in the past, telling him to forget it, to become less than he could be.

Kayode straightened in his chair, smiled, and nodded. "Thank you," he said.

After we had made our arrangements for church the next morning and said good night to Olufemi and his family, we settled down to sleep, all four of us in the living room. We were tired, but sleep did not come quickly. Tani and Austin were making us laugh, and the more we talked, the clearer it became that we were all feeling excited about this new adventure that lay ahead. Despite Dallas, we were ready to believe that good things were just around the corner.

When the boys finally gave in to sleep, I asked Kayode about his conversation with Olufemi. I wanted to know what he felt about no longer seeing himself as the kind of man who was a CEO or chairman of the board.

I could see Kayode smiling in the semidarkness. "I will do whatever I have to do to move my family forward."

"Even if that means taking on a job that you would not ever dream of doing back in Nigeria?"

"Whatever it takes. No job can be beneath me if it means I can provide for the people I love."

21 | A REALLY GOOD DAY

TANI ————————

SUNDAY, DECEMBER 17, 2017

Let me tell you why it was maybe one of the best days ever.

First, we all slept in the same room. Austin, Mom, and I woke up in the morning when Dad started snoring so loud that it sounded like there was an elephant outside. That was funny, and it's hard to have a bad day when you wake up laughing.

Then we went to church. It wasn't like church in Dallas, where I had to sit next to one of my cousins, and they would poke me and hit me if they got bored. It wasn't like church back in Nigeria either because there were no metal detectors. It wasn't even like a church at all. It was just a regular house on a regular street, and the church was down in the basement.

Dad wore a suit and Mom wore one of her bright dresses, and the tiny basement was full of people dressed just like them. Everyone was smiling and saying hi, and nobody poked me or hit me, and nobody checked anybody for weapons. When one of the pastors started calling out Bible verses and asking all the kids to look them up as fast as they could, I even won a couple of times. Nobody gave me any bad looks. They just carried on smiling and treating us all well.

The main pastor was named Pastor Phillip, and he was extra nice. It was his basement we were meeting in, and he made everyone feel super welcome. He was so tall that he would have hit his head on the ceiling if he jumped up. And even though everyone else in the room was friendly, Pastor Phillip had the biggest smile of all. He told us that he was from the same part of Nigeria where we were from and that we were welcome. I liked him a lot.

After we'd finished church, we ate platefuls of jollof rice and fried turkey. I love Nigerian food, and they'd cooked it just the same way Mom does.

But there was something else that made the day even better. While we were in church, it started snowing.

I'd seen snow before but only on TV. Mom and Dad and Austin were the same. So when we'd finished eating and helped clean up, we all ran outside.

The first weird thing I noticed was that I didn't feel as cold as I thought I would. Every time you see someone on TV in the snow, it always looks like they're really, really cold. I got pretty hot when I was running around in the front yard of the church. And my hands went numb, which meant that they stopped feeling anything at all.

The other weird thing was the way it felt. Snow is just frozen water, so I suppose I should not have been surprised, but I was. My pants and hair and shoes were soon wet just like I'd been out in the rain.

But the best thing was how much fun we had. Mom and Dad were with us outside, and they were laughing just as loud as Austin and me. We were patting the snow down and kicking it. We were making it into balls and throwing it. One of the kids from church showed Austin and me how to make snow angels. It was so, so great.

The only bad part was when my hands stopped feeling numb and started feeling like they were on fire. I went back inside then. It took a long time to get warm.

Church was over, but Pastor Phillip told Mom and Dad that we could stay at his house as long as we liked. He had a lot of other people staying in his house as well, so the only room we could sleep in was the basement, where we had all met for church. It was cold down there, and there wasn't any carpet on the floor. It was just bare concrete. But Pastor Phillip brought down so many blankets and pillows and cushions that we were able to get kind of warm.

Before we went to bed, we did what we always do and prayed for a half hour. Mom and Dad usually start, and then Austin and I join in. We sing some songs, then say sorry to God, and then thank Him for all the good things He has given us. There was a lot to thank God for that night.

When we'd finished praying, we settled down to sleep. So the day ended just like it began. Mom and Dad and Austin and I were all in the same room, lying in our beds and laughing. We were talking about the snow and how much fun it was and how kind Pastor Phillip was and how friendly everyone in church had been that day.

Then Austin asked a question that had just come into my mind as well. He said, "Dad? What's going to happen tomorrow?"

Dad said, "Listen to me." Whenever he says that, Austin and I know that whatever words Dad is about to say are super important. And when he talks like this, I always like it. It makes me feel awake and safe and warm inside. Even if I'm tired and have lots of questions that I can't answer and I'm feeling cold—like I was in the basement or out in the snow—when Dad says that we need to listen, I listen.

Dad said, "Tomorrow will be a great day. Tomorrow we begin our new life here in New York."

22 | LONGING FOR SHELTER

KAYODE ————

Early on Monday morning, while it was still dark outside, Pastor Phillip drove us through the snow to the Bronx and a place that he said was an intake center run by the Department of Homeless Services. He showed us inside, explained a little of what we could expect, and told us that he would be available to help at any point in the day if we needed him.

"These are good people," he said as he prepared to go. "They can help you."

We had first met him less than twenty-four hours earlier, but I already knew that I trusted Pastor Phillip completely. I had seen enough of him to know that he was a man of integrity and a man of kindness. We exchanged numbers and agreed to keep in contact.

Even at a little after seven o'clock in the morning, it was busy inside the Prevention Assistance and Temporary Housing intake center, which everyone calls PATH. None of us spoke much as we waited in line to be seen. Even Tani, who usually would have kept up an endless stream of questions, was silent. We were all nervous, all looking around, trying to make sense of this strange new place.

Pastor Phillip had told us that PATH was a service run by the government, but if he had not, I would not have believed it. It looked nothing like the type of services run by the government back in Nigeria. The building was modern, clean, and bright. Instead of an administrative office, it reminded me much more of an airport terminal.

Yet one thing was familiar. The waiting. We spent hours sitting on plastic benches, waiting for our name to be called. Only when someone called "Aid-Woom" or "A-Dumely" could we approach the designated desk, answer whatever questions we were asked, and walk away with several new forms to fill out before taking them to a different department on a different floor, where we would have to wait again until we were called.

Every two or three hours, Pastor Phillip phoned me.

"How are you?" he would ask. "How's it going there? Who have you seen now? What kind of questions are they asking? Do you need me to come over?"

Each time he called I told him what I could, though most of the time there was not much to report. We were waiting, trusting that everything would work out.

Twelve hours after we arrived at PATH, after we had seen so many different people and sat at so many different desks, we received the news that we had been hoping for all day. We had been offered accommodations.

I called Pastor Phillip. He cheered and thanked God.

"We have been told that we are going to be housed in a shelter. Is that like a tent?"

"No," said Pastor Phillip. "A shelter is good. You will be with lots of other people who are homeless. There will be staff there who can help you find schools for the boys, find work, and progress your asylum claim."

"That's good."

"Yes, it is. Did they tell you where it is yet?"

"Yes," I said, looking at the piece of paper. I did not recognize the address. "Where is Manhattan? Is it near Queens? My wife and I hope so. We really want to be near you and the church."

"Manhattan? They're putting you in a shelter in Manhattan? That's good, my friend."

"It is? Why? Is it near Queens?"

"No. It's better than Queens, believe me. Manhattan is the center. You're going to be in the heart of the greatest city on earth! What's the address?"

I looked again. "Thirtieth Street, Park Avenue."

There was a small pause, then I heard him exclaim, "Whoa!"

"Is that good too?"

"Is it good? Yes, it's good, Kayode! It's really good. God is blessing you mightily. Park Avenue is the best road in the whole city. And you're going to be living there. Praise God!"

We waited another hour before the bus arrived to drive us from the PATH office to the shelter. We were all tired by that point, and perhaps a little nervous, too, as we sat with our bags on our laps and by our feet. But as we drove along the bottom of great canyons of concrete and glass and bright lights, I remembered something that my father would say when I was younger. It was good advice, and I wanted to pass it on to my sons.

"Know where you come from," I said. "Whatever lies ahead in the shelter on this Park Avenue, let us not forget who we are or where we come from. Let us choose always to be polite and respectful, to be kind and generous. Let us not forget that we are Yoruba, that we are the grandson and great-grandsons of a king. Let us show our appreciation for this blessing by being a blessing to others. Do you agree?"

"Amen," said Oluwatoyin, Austin, and Tani. "Amen! Amen!"

23 | SAFE AND SECURE AT LAST

OLUWATOYIN ──────

I don't know what I had imagined the shelter would look like, but as we walked through the glass doors and stood in the hotel lobby, with its golden lights and comfortable armchairs, I was sure for a moment that we had entered the wrong building.

"Excuse me," I said to the young man at the front desk. "We're trying to find the homeless shelter, but we've been given the wrong address. Can you help us?"

He smiled. "You're in the right place. Take the elevator to the seventh floor, turn right, and you'll find the office at the end of the hallway. They'll help you."

As we stood in front of the giant mirror and waited for the elevator, we were all staring wide-eyed and struggling to believe it. Dallas had been so different from Nigeria, but this was another world altogether. The buildings were taller, the lights were brighter, and now this: a home in a hotel provided by the government. If this wasn't the greatest city on earth, I couldn't imagine anything better.

It wasn't quite as clean and smart up on the seventh floor as it was down in the lobby, but we barely noticed. We were still stunned that a place like this even existed.

We found the office and met Jacki, who was in charge that night. She gave us papers to sign and explained the rules of the shelter.

"First, curfew is 9:00 p.m. If you ain't signed in by then for three nights running, then you're out. Second, no alcohol. If we find that you've brought any alcohol into your room or anywhere in the facility, you're gone."

Kayode and I glanced at each other. The curfew was no problem, and neither of us were big on drinking. The news that nobody else in the shelter would have alcohol was a relief.

"It's the same with smoking, drugs, or using anything like an iron or a stove in your room. You can't do that. It's forbidden, and you've got to make sure your boys understand that too. If we catch you, you're gone."

More nodding, this time from Austin and Tani as well.

"We serve three meals a day, but those times are strict. If you miss the mealtime, you miss the meal. And every time you come in and every time you leave, you have to sign in and out right here in this office. And you don't hold a key to your room. When you come in, you have to wait for one of us to take you to your room and unlock it for you. That way you know that your room is safe. You got all that?"

We nodded, but Jacki was busy looking at some papers on her desk. "Every Sunday afternoon you're going to see your case manager from PATH at five. You can't be late for that, you understand? And you're here for ten days. If you're good people and behave well, you'll be invited to stay until PATH finds you a house of your own."

Jacki took us to our two rooms, one on the fifth floor and one on the fourth. I settled the boys into theirs, then Kayode joined us to pray.

There was so much to thank God for.

That night Kayode and I held hands across the narrow gap that separated our single beds. The room was only large enough for the beds and a chest of drawers, but it had a small bathroom, a window, and a lock on the door. We were safe, we were secure, and we finally had a space that was our own, even if it was for only ten days.

"Wow," said Kayode as he looked out of the window at the buildings towering above us. "What kind of country pays for its homeless people to live in a hotel?"

"A country that knows how to care for its people," I said. "A good country, run by kind people."

While Yoruba people are famous for their kindness and hospitality, our government would never offer such support to people who could not repay them. Corruption, a lack of resources, the wide gulf that exists between rich and poor—there are so many reasons why there are no homeless shelters set in the wealthiest streets of Nigeria. There are no homeless shelters in any city of the country. None at all. If you are homeless, your only hope is your family.

Kayode sighed. "Can you imagine anything like this ever happening in Nigeria?"

Neither of us could.

24 | SCHOOL IN A NEW CITY

TANI ————————

The people who run America really like for you to go to school. I know this because when we got to Dallas, Austin and I started school maybe three or four days after we arrived.

In New York, it happened even quicker.

We woke up on the second morning in The Hotel. Mom and Dad and everybody who worked there called it The Shelter, but I call it The Hotel because if you go to the corner of Thirtieth Street and Park Avenue, you won't see any sign that says "Shelter." You'll just see a hotel.

So Austin and I woke up early in the morning and rode the elevator down to Mom and Dad's room on the floor below. Then we all went up to the seventh floor to eat breakfast. I didn't recognize much of the food they had on the tables, but Mom helped me choose a muffin and a juice box. And that's when Dad told us that we were going to visit a school that day. I stopped being hungry for my muffin.

I do like school. I like it because I like asking questions, and in school, if you like asking questions, the teachers usually are happy about it and tell your parents that you're a good student. But when Dad said we were going to visit a school that morning, I was not so sure that I was ready. Dallas was different from Nigeria, but New York was even more different. In Dallas the schools looked a lot more like they did in Nigeria, with trees and sports fields and lots of space to run around. All the schools we had walked or driven by in New York were strange. The buildings were tall with really high fences, and I couldn't see trees around any of them. If the schools were different outside, I guessed that they would be different inside as well.

Later that morning Mom was walking with Austin and me to visit our two new schools. She said, "I know that it is not always easy to go into a new school, but do you remember what Dad said the night we arrived at the shelter?"

I did remember because it was one of those things that Dad says *a lot*. But I like it. I think it's good advice, so I told Mom, "Yes. He said, 'Know where you come from.'"

She said, "That's right. You both will do well if you remember that. If anyone offends you, don't talk back. Report it to your teacher or the supervisor at recess, or me if you need to. Just don't disrespect anybody, even if they are younger or older. And always be the first to apologize. Sorry goes a long way. And if someone says sorry to you and you're still complaining, what else do you want? It's a powerful word; let it be in your mouth."

Mom had said the same words when we started school in Dallas. I guess she probably said the same words when we started school in Nigeria, but I didn't mind her or Dad repeating themselves. They always give good advice. I know that I can trust them.

I started school the next day, but I did not need to apologize for anything or report anybody being mean to me. The teachers were kind, and the other kids were all friendly. By the end of the day, I had made a bunch of new friends. A lot of them asked me questions about Nigeria and Dallas, and I told them what I could remember.

I asked them a lot of questions, too, like, "What do you do at recess?" and "Do you like all the teachers the same, or are some nicer than others?" I listened carefully to all their answers and tried to remember every word. It was hard because some of the games they talked about I'd never heard of, and I didn't know the names of the teachers yet. But there was one answer they gave that I did not have to struggle to remember. It was the answer to my question, "What's your favorite subject?" And this is what one of them said:

"Chess."

25 | TIRED AND HAPPY

It is my belief that when you are faced with difficulties, your struggles will be multiplied if you give yourself over to stress. And if you act as if you are the only one who can solve your problems, then your prospects will become even worse.

That is not the way my father taught me to live. He showed me the value of patience and taught me the importance of stopping, waiting, and listening before deciding what course of action to take. "Do that," he told me frequently, "and eventually things will put themselves right. You might have to wait a long time, but when the right help comes, you will know."

Even though Austin and Tani insisted on calling the shelter The Hotel, Oluwatoyin and I saw it for what it was: a place for people who had reached some of the lowest points in their lives. But even though we had been wealthy in Nigeria, we did not believe that we were above our fellow residents on the fourth to seventh floors. Nor did we believe that we were inferior because of the fact that we were immigrants who were still ignorant of much of the new culture surrounding us. We were in the same position.

We were grateful for the help of a generous government and looking for the change that was to come.

The only difference between us and some of the other residents was the fact that, for us, the day we first walked into the building near the corner of Thirtieth Street and Park Avenue we knew that the change we had been waiting for had finally arrived. We moved into the shelter in December. In many ways I had spent the whole year waiting. Waiting for Boko Haram to either attack us or to forget about us. Waiting for a solution to arrive that would show us the way forward. Waiting for life in Dallas to improve. Waiting for Grandma to change her mind. It had given me a lot of time to think and to listen and to ask what lay ahead for us as a family.

The minute I first met him, I knew that Pastor Phillip was the help we had been waiting for. He encouraged us, loved us, provided for us. And because he had helped many other Nigerian families who moved to New York, he was able to guide us to other sources of help, like PATH. After all that waiting, Pastor Phillip arrived in our lives at just the right time.

So I was not surprised when other things started to change as soon as we moved into the shelter. The boys started at new schools, we started to make progress with our claim for asylum, and with each day that passed and each conversation we had with the people living and working in the shelter, we felt more and more at home.

The biggest change for me was work. Pastor Phillip had explained that while I was waiting for my work authorization to be granted, I could look for work but only for a certain kind of job. It would have to be unskilled, low wage, and without any of the benefits that I would expect once I had my Social Security number.

This was very good news. "I do not mind what I do," I had said to Pastor Phillip, "just as long as I do something."

Less than one week after we moved into the shelter, I rode the subway north for almost an hour, caught up in the early evening crowds. Pastor Phillip had put me in contact with a friend of his, and I was heading to work. I knew that it was not a glamorous job, but the fact that I would be able to earn money to provide for my family was all the dignity I needed.

The job was simple. I was a night cleaner in the kitchen of a large restaurant in the Bronx. I was to work from 9:00 p.m. until 7:00 a.m., six nights a week, and for that I would be paid a little more than six dollars an hour.

Because I was new, I was given the jobs nobody else wanted. I washed 250 pans. I loaded countless plates into the industrial dishwasher. And once the oven had cooled down, I had to dismantle it, clean off the fat and grease that had accumulated throughout the day, and wash the floor. The oven was made of iron, and the pieces I had to lift off and clean were so heavy that I feared what would happen to either of my feet if my grip slipped and I dropped them.

I returned back to the shelter the next morning. I was so exhausted that I was ready to fall asleep almost as soon as I lay on the bed.

Oluwatoyin sat down beside me. She looked concerned. "Are you okay?"

"I am tired, but how can I not be happy? We are alive and well. We are safe from harm. And tonight I will have another opportunity to go to work and keep my family moving forward."

My eyes were growing heavy.

My back was sore.

With each breath I could feel myself sinking deeper and deeper into the bed.

The last thing I remember was looking at her smiling back at me.

26 | A TASTE OF HOME

OLUWATOYIN ─────────

Every day there were so many things that reminded us of the generosity of the American government. I never once ran the shower and failed to get hot water, the lights never went out, and our rooms were free of charge. The staff was happy to help us with any question we had, and at the end of every school day, the boys were always able to talk with excitement about what they had learned. We were blessed to be in the shelter, and we knew it.

There was only one thing that we wanted to change. We were given three meals each day up on the seventh floor, and the food they served was not the kind we were used to. The boys were happy to try any new dish once, but it soon became clear to me that they were just not comfortable with the typical American diet. They either found the food too bland or they could not stomach the amount of dairy in the cooking. So when I realized that the only things they were happily eating were cookies and muffins, I decided to do something.

There was no way that we could cook at the shelter, but thanks to Kayode's job, we had some money, and I was able to take Pastor Phillip up on an offer he had made us. As a Nigerian, he knew the importance of food to our family, and he had told me that I was welcome to return to his house whenever I wanted to use his kitchen.

The challenge was finding the ingredients to make the dishes that the boys liked—traditional Nigerian soups, curries, and rice full of beans, yams, and other good things. I looked in the stores that I walked by on the way to and from Tani's school, but none of them sold what I needed. I asked around, and pretty soon it was clear that if I wanted to find good African food stores, Manhattan was the wrong place to be looking. If I wanted African food, I needed to look where the Africans lived, and that was back in Queens, near Pastor Phillip's house.

And so I started a new routine. On Sundays I would stay after church, and on Wednesdays and Fridays I would head east and return to Queens. It took more than two hours and a combination of three trains and one bus, but it was worth it. Spending three or four hours in the kitchen, filling the air with steam and spice and the smells that reminded me of home, never failed to satisfy me. I was thousands of miles from my homeland, but I had not left it behind.

After I'd shopped, cooked, and cleaned the kitchen, I made the long journey back to Manhattan. I was always tired at the end of these days, and the shopping cart I pulled behind me was heavy. But it was worth it. Even on the days when it had been snowing and I had to fight to keep the cart from tipping over, it was still worth it. Sitting on the bus or the train, feeling the heat glowing gently from the still-warm Tupperware containers bursting with meals, I was grateful for the chance to feed my family.

Each night when I returned home from these cooking days, Kayode, Austin, and Tani would be so excited to see what I had made that they'd listen in silence as I announced each container when I removed it from the cart. After we'd chosen which dish we were going to eat that night, the rest would go into our refrigerator (the cold air on the fire escape outside our window). I'd open up the chosen meal, still slightly warm from that afternoon's cooking, and all three of them would sit there, eyes wide, mouths open, as if I were a magician performing right before their eyes.

The sacrifice of my time and energy was worth it a thousand times over.

27 | MY FIRST CHESS LESSON

TANI ——————

People are kind.

Sometimes you find someone who can be mean to you, but most of the time people are kind. I know this because of what happened at The Hotel.

One morning I was waiting for Mom and Austin to get off the elevator and sign out when a lady named Miss Maria looked out from the office down the hall and said, "Hey, Tani. Come here."

Dad and Mom liked Miss Maria a lot. They were always asking her questions and getting her advice on what to do about things. Every week there would be maybe four or five times when they'd be talking about something and one of them would say, "We need to ask Miss Maria about that." They'd save up their questions until the next time they saw her, and then she'd give them the answers.

I had my own reasons for liking Miss Maria. Every morning that she was working at The Hotel, she'd bring a doughnut. One day she'd give it to me, and the next day she'd give it to Austin.

That's why I was waiting on my own at the elevator. It was my turn to get the doughnut.

But when Miss Maria called me down and I saw her sitting at her desk, I couldn't see any doughnuts at all. I could see a box though. It was big, and the lid was off. Inside was a really nice pair of sneakers.

She smiled and said, "I've got something else for you today. You remember how I was telling you that I've got a son who's a year older than you?"

"Yes," I said.

Miss Maria said, "Well, his grandma bought him these, and they don't fit. I thought they might fit you. Do you want to try them on?"

I don't know much about sneakers, but I knew that I liked these a lot. They were the whitest pair I'd ever seen, and they looked like the kind that if you wore them when you were playing basketball, you'd probably be able to jump an extra ten feet in the air because of them. So I nodded and said, "Yes, please, Miss Maria."

I had just gotten them on my feet when Mom came in. Miss Maria explained about her son and his grandma, and Mom was saying thank you so much and smiling so big that I thought she was going to explode.

But not everyone in The Hotel was nice like Miss Maria.

If Dad had gone to work early and Mom was still at Pastor Phillip's house cooking for us, then Austin would come get me from school, and we would walk back to The Hotel together. Sometimes there were the kind of people living there who were annoying and would get into our business if they saw us riding the elevator on our own. They'd say things like, "Your parents aren't home? Tell your parents to come on home!" Austin taught me how to stay quiet and not look them in the eye and wait until they finished. He told me that they'd always get bored soon enough if we didn't give them a reaction. He was right every time.

Sometimes the same people who were getting in our faces when we were alone would get thrown out because they had been caught with beer in their rooms or they'd missed the curfew three times running. I always thought that was dumb because the rules were written really clearly on the office door, and so every time you went to sign in or sign out or to get your meals, you saw them all there in a long list. And because it was cold outside,

I wondered what would happen to these people. Did they have another hotel to go to? I hoped so.

One of the kindest people of all is Austin. He is really patient and good at teaching me things. Even if he didn't quite get everything right with chess when we were in Nigeria, I'm still glad that he helped me learn.

He teaches me other things too. Like basketball. He's *so much* taller than me, so he's way better than I am, but he takes time to show me how to get better.

It's the same with math. Austin's really good at math, and he helps me with mine. He tells me things that they don't talk about in school, which is really cool. Like percentages. When he first started telling me about them, I was confused, but he worked hard to make sure that I understood.

"Think about it this way," he said. "We can work out what percentage of people in The Hotel are unkind and what percentage are kind."

I said, "How?"

He said, "There are four floors in The Hotel and twenty rooms on each floor. With 2 people in each room, that makes the total number of people living in The Hotel 160. Out of all the people we know here, how many are not kind?"

I had to think about that for a while, but I could only count 4 people who would say things that I didn't like.

Austin said that he agreed and showed me that 4 people out of 160 was just 2.5 percent.

"That's a low number," I said.

He said, "Yes, and it means that 97.5 percent of people in here are kind."

We both agreed that was a lot of kindness.

In Dallas the percentage of people who were not nice to us was a lot higher. It was maybe 80 percent not nice and 20 percent nice. Figuring that out made it even easier to ignore anyone who was weird with us in The Hotel.

My school was P.S. 116, and it is on East Thirty-Third Street. It takes ten minutes to walk there from The Hotel, and the percentage of not nice people there was maybe the same as The Hotel but probably lower. There were a lot more people at school than there were at The Hotel, and I didn't know all of them. Mom has always told Austin and me to be polite and friendly and to say sorry if we do anything wrong and not to keep being mean to someone if they've apologized to us. If you act like that at school, then hardly anyone will have a problem with you.

But in the same way that Miss Maria was the nicest person out of everyone in The Hotel, there was one teacher at P.S. 116 who was even nicer than the others. His name is Coach Shawn Martinez. He didn't buy me doughnuts or give me sneakers, but he gave me something even better.

He taught me how to play chess.

When I went into the first lesson with Coach Shawn one day before recess, I thought I knew how to play chess. I remembered most of what Austin had taught me when we were in Nigeria and had made our set out of paper. But even before Coach Shawn started talking, I could tell that Austin's chess wasn't much like Coach Shawn's chess. There were no little squares of paper anywhere. Instead, there were all these little statues that I really wanted to pick up.

I didn't pick them up.

I was too busy looking at Coach Shawn. I didn't know back then what a typical chess coach would look like, but I knew that Coach Shawn didn't look like any of my schoolteachers. He was wearing the kind of sneakers that look like they'd make you jump *really* high. And he talked different too. He didn't sound like he was trying to test us or trick us or work out what we didn't know. He sounded like he was sharing his most favorite secrets ever. He sounded like he loved chess more than anything in the world.

I had to listen so hard because Coach Shawn started talking about things I didn't understand. *Pawns. Openings. Checkmate.* All of these words were new to me, and none of them made any sense at all. But I wanted them to. I liked the way the pieces felt in my hand, and I liked the way they looked when they were all lined up at the start. When I heard the words *chess is battle*, it kind of made sense to me.

I was put with another boy who hadn't been playing long, but I didn't understand what to do. When it was my turn to go, I'd pick up a piece and move it, but the boy would shake his head and say things like "You can't do that" or "Illegal!" So I ended up copying whatever move he had done and hoping that it would work.

Soon he said, "Checkmate!" I looked at him and said, "What's that?" He said, "It's over. I won."

Right then there was a part of me that didn't want to play chess ever again. But there was another part of me that really, really did. I liked being there, and I liked the way the room felt. It was kind of like a library and kind of like a church. So when Coach Shawn came over and smiled at me, I smiled back. I said, "I don't know how to do it. But I want to."

He said, "Don't worry. Everyone here has been playing for at least three months. They know more than you do right now, but we can change that. I'm going to show you how each piece moves. If you pay attention and remember what they do, you might be able to play in about two weeks."

I paid attention. I watched him pick up each piece and show me the way it was allowed to move. I made my brain remember everything he said. I locked it inside of me.

"You got all that?" asked Coach Shawn when he put down the last piece.

I nodded and said yes.

"You want me to go over anything?"

"No."

28 | GOD CAN RESCUE US

KAYODE ————

When we were living in the shelter, I often remembered the day in the market in Ado Ekiti when I first set eyes on Oluwatoyin. When I was lying on the bed after working all night, trying to ignore the many different pains that were troubling my body, those memories became my medicine.

Every morning it was the same. I would arrive back at the shelter, too tired to eat, too tired to shower or change out of my clothes. Once I had signed in and returned to the room, I would simply lie down on the bed and be asleep within minutes. Hours later, before the boys finished school, I would wake up in pain.

It was always the same parts of my body that hurt. My shoulders. My feet. My back. But the worst of the pain was always in my hands. They would be bent like claws, and before I could even get out of bed, I would have to spend several minutes stretching them back to life.

The stabbing ache that ran through my body was not the only problem I had to deal with. The room itself was so small that if you weren't standing in the gap between the beds or in the bathroom, you had to be sitting or lying on the bed. I was back in the same place I had been in Dallas—locked away and lying down.

I did not like feeling trapped like this. I did not like it at all. And so I thought about Oluwatoyin a lot. Remembering how we had met, fallen in love, and watched our family grow together was like medicine for my aching body and troubled mind.

Even better than thinking about Oluwatoyin was being with her. That is why, even though I loved to be able to eat the food she made, I liked it so much when she was not cooking at Pastor Phillip's house. When she was in our room in the shelter, sitting on her bed, reading or resting, smiling at me as I woke up, then at least we could talk. Sometimes we would talk about big, important issues, sometimes just about the ordinary facts of the day. I did not mind at all. I just liked listening to the sound of her voice.

Oluwatoyin would often tell me about the things she had seen on her journeys to and from Queens. She has always been drawn to people, and soon after she started traveling to Pastor Phillip's kitchen, she told me she had seen a white man and a white woman who were homeless trying to keep warm in the train station.

"They were begging," she said. "They looked as though they had been begging all their lives."

She saw them again when she next made the trip. That night she told me how she had spoken to the homeless woman, asking if she had heard of PATH.

"Had she?" I asked.

"No. So I encouraged them to google it and visit. I said that whatever their problem, PATH could help."

The next time Oluwatoyin came home, pulling her shopping cart full of delicious-smelling meals, she told me that the couple was still there.

I was distracted by thoughts of the food we would soon be eating, but Oluwatoyin wanted to talk.

"They are still begging."

"Who?"

"The white couple that I spoke to about PATH. I saw them in the station again today. I walked over to talk with them and see if I could help, but they both avoided me."

"They did not want to talk to you?"

"No. They are still begging. It is as if they are trapped."

Trapped was exactly how I felt. I knew that Oluwatoyin struggled in her own way as well, that she wanted to be a great mother to the boys and a great wife to me, but there was a heavy physical cost in doing so. And I knew that for some people the cost was too much to make these choices, that begging was less painful than the battles they would have to take on to put their lives back on the right track again.

We met so many good people at the shelter and so many good people at PATH. Some people were asylum seekers like us; others were not. Some had faced tragedy; some had been the victims of bad fortune. But regardless of what had caused them to become homeless, the ones who were moving forward in life were the people who refused to be trapped. Like us, they would fight to push forward every day. They would work hard. They would never give up.

Of all the conversations that Oluwatoyin had with New Yorkers, the ones that left her feeling saddened or sorrowful were few. We were both aware how far we were from home and how different the culture was in New York compared to Nigeria, but we were both surprised by how many times we saw displays of kindness and respect on the streets. Oluwatoyin and I would trade stories of young people helping the old with their heavy bags or commuters volunteering their seats for others on the subway. Despite all the crowds and the chaos and the wealth and the poverty, New Yorkers could be kind and generous to each other.

Every evening, after we had eaten dinner and before I left for work, we would all gather in either the boys' room or ours to talk, read the Bible, encourage each other, and pray. It was a ritual that Oluwatoyin and I had been practicing ever since we had married, but the threat from Boko Haram had certainly made us pray longer and louder. So had the struggles in Dallas and the new start in New York.

One night Oluwatoyin was telling us about how she had been talking with one of the women who worked as a security guard for the main hotel downstairs.

"I told her about the words of Isaiah 60, 'Arise, for the light has come.' She has been looking so down lately, and I want her to know that there is hope, even in the darkness. I wanted to encourage her to keep believing in God, to know that God can do many things for her, and that no matter how great the obstacle we face, God can rescue us."

She paused. We all did. A few seconds stretched toward a minute.

We all needed to hear her words and take them as our own.

Soon we started singing and clapping, and then we moved to close the way we always did, with every one of us getting ready to say amen. But first Oluwatoyin reminded us of the important truth, proclaiming loudly, "No matter how great the obstacle we face, God can rescue us."

"A-men," we called. "Amen! Amen!"

The doors at the shelter were not thick. From outside we heard the sound of someone calling out, "A-men!"

My cleaning job was tough. I knew I could not last long at it. Eventually I would have to find something else, something that did not leave me in agony at the end of every day. But all that would happen in good time. There was something more important for me to do. I had to choose not to fear. I had to choose not to look at my twisted hands or the way the walls in our room were so close together.

I cannot express how grateful I am for my wife. I know that I am not a lazy person, I know that I can work hard, and I know that this country offers opportunity to the people who are prepared to keep working, to keep moving. But my sweat and determination is not enough. Without Oluwatoyin's encouragement, I would not be able to continue.

29 | KNOWING THE RIGHT MOVES

TANI ————————

I tried really hard to remember everything Coach Shawn told me about the way the different pieces move. Pawns were easy. So were the king and the queen. I thought that knights looked really strange, so I never had any problem with those. But I got confused between bishops and rooks.

That's why I was feeling nervous at the start of my second lesson with Coach Shawn. I was worried that he would want to check to see how well I had been listening to him the week before, and that if I got any wrong, he'd be upset, or it would hurt my grades somehow.

Right before the start of the lesson when everyone was getting their boards set up, he came over and started talking to me. "Hey, Tani. You okay?"

I nodded and said, "Yes, Coach Shawn." I was really worried now because there were other people watching. And when Coach Shawn asked if I remembered any of the pieces and how they moved, I told him that I did. I picked up each piece and showed him what it did, but when I got to the bishops and rooks, my head felt really hot, and I couldn't remember anything at all about them.

Coach Shawn was looking at me. He was smiling. Then he said, "Tani, that's good. Really good. Did anyone help you remember them?"

I shook my head.

He kept looking at me. His smile got bigger. Then he held out his hand, gave me a fist bump, and called everyone to pay attention, as the lesson was going to begin.

"All right, all right, all right," he said. "Listen up. I've got a riddle for you. You ready?"

Everyone said, "Yes, Coach Shawn!"

And he said, "Okay, so can you guys name something that has four legs in the morning, two in the afternoon, and three at night?"

Almost everyone put their hand up because they thought they could guess the answer. Coach Shawn picked people to call out, and some of the answers were really funny. Someone said an elephant! Someone else said a bed. My favorite was "a rocket that got busted." Coach Shawn was laughing at us all, but nobody got it right. When everyone who had their hand up had tried to guess, Coach Shawn said, "Okay, okay, I'll tell you. It's a human being. When you're a baby you crawl, so you've got four legs. Then when you're older, and it's like the afternoon of your life, you walk with two feet. When you get real old, you're going to need a cane, and so that's why humans have three legs in the evening."

Some people were confused and didn't get it, but I did. I thought it was clever.

Next, Coach Shawn started talking about chess, and I listened so hard. I even moved places so I could be right in the front row and able to see him up close. I wanted to make sure I heard every word he said.

"We've been working for three months now, and I know you all know the moves of the pieces, but I've got to tell you that knowing the moves is not enough. The concept of the game is a lot deeper. If you want to be good at chess, you've got to learn how to make good decisions."

Then he said something strange. "Raise your hand if you know how to cross the street."

I put a hand up in the air. I looked around and everyone else had too.

Coach Shawn nodded. Then he said, "Right. Is it simple or difficult to cross the street?"

We all called out, "It's simple!"

"Okay, but if one day you forget what to do when you're crossing the street, and you forget to look both ways and make that mistake, what could happen to you?"

I had my hand up high. Mom had been talking to me a lot about crossing the street ever since we'd moved to The Hotel because the roads in New York are *a lot* busier than they are in Dallas or most places in Nigeria. When Coach Shawn called on me to answer, I said, "You'd be hit by a car, and you might die."

He said, "Yes, that's right, Tani. Even a simple thing like crossing the street can have really bad consequences for your life. And that's like chess. You might think that since you're just making a simple move you can make it fast and not think about it carefully, but you can end up in so much trouble. You've got to think the consequences through. You've got to think deep. Otherwise you're going to end up in trouble."

I liked everything that Coach Shawn said. Everything.

That's when I knew that I really wanted to be a chess player.

30 | AN IMPOSSIBLY EXPENSIVE ACTIVITY

OLUWATOYIN ───────

Ever since I met Kayode I have known him to work hard. But after just two weeks of washing dishes, he wasn't just tired—he was exhausted.

Naturally, I wanted to help him. If I was in the room with him during the day, I'd make sure that I kept quiet and let him sleep as long as he could. There were other things I did as well. I worked hard to keep any burdens from him that he didn't need to worry about. If he asked me how I was doing, I would tell him "fine," even if I was feeling trapped or tired or sad about the way things had ended back in Dallas. I tried my hardest to keep all that to myself, pull myself together, and get over whatever it was that was trying to weigh me down.

But when Tani came home from school saying that he wanted to enroll in the after-school chess program and showed me a letter that said it would cost $330 for one semester, I didn't know what to do.

Telling Kayode about it was a bad idea that I wanted to rule out at once. I knew that $330 was an impossible amount of money for us to spend on an after-school activity that ran for only two and a half hours each week.

Kayode's job was bringing in a maximum of $300 each week, and we were spending more than half of it on food and travel. The rest we used for essentials. What was left each week was never more than a few dollars.

But there was something about the way Tani spoke about the club and a man named Coach Shawn that made me want to think a little harder and not just dismiss the idea out of hand.

Tani had been talking about it all nonstop, and not just in the way Tani usually speaks about whatever he is passionate about at the time. On almost every walk to or from school, he told me about chess in a way that made it clear to me he was really thinking deeply about it.

"Coach Shawn says that some people like chess because it's competitive. They like winning, and if you do like forty or fifty chess puzzles each week and go to practice and work really hard, you will get better. But some people like it because maybe they're not good at sports or have never been on a team, and so when they join the chess program, they're part of a real team that goes to tournaments and competes together. Some people like chess because they like the way they have to do what he calls 'deep thinking'—"

"Wait, Tani," I said, grabbing his backpack and stopping him from stepping into the road. "The light's not green yet."

"Deep thinking is when you have to make your brain really concentrate harder than you've ever made it concentrate before and imagine all the possible moves that could follow when you make a certain move. Coach Shawn says that with practice you can do deep thinking so good that you can see four or five moves ahead."

"Okay. So which of those reasons is the main one behind your wanting to play?"

Tani thought hard. "All of them."

"All of them?"

"Yes. Coach Shawn says that chess is not a game that you just pick up. He says you've got to understand it all, every part of it, and to do that, you have to make sacrifices. But if you do that and work hard, then you can go far."

I decided that the best way to talk to Kayode about it was simply to tell him the facts. So one afternoon when he had finished eating, I told him about Tani, Coach Shawn, and the question of whether we could talk about the $330 it would cost for Tani to enroll.

Kayode looked at me. He'd slept for hours, but he still looked tired. "We have no money!"

"I know we don't."

"Can't he do something free instead?"

"Free? Maybe," I said. "Let me see."

I didn't talk to Tani about enrolling in a different course. Not yet, at least. I'd seen something on the letter about scholarships, and I hoped that there might be a way of reducing the fee a little. The only other problem was that the letter Tani had brought back about the program wasn't signed by Coach Shawn but by someone named Coach Russ. I'd never heard the name Russ before, so I did not know whether it was a man's or a woman's name. I hoped that he or she would not be offended by my opening.

FROM: Oluwatoyin Adewumi
TO: Impact Coaching Network
DATE: Thu, Feb 1, 2018, 10:03 AM

Good morning Mr./Ms. Russ Makofsky, Head of Chess Program,

I am Mrs. Adewumi, a mother to Tanitoluwa Adewumi one of your students in 2nd grade, Class 2-304.

He is interested in the Chess Program, which he will like to be participating in.

I learnt the program held in the school every Thursday from 2:35–5:00pm. Please, I will like to know about the Scholarship Program for his interest.

Thank you.

Oluwatoyin Adewumi

Coach Russ replied almost immediately:

FROM: Impact Coaching Network
TO: Oluwatoyin Adewumi
DATE: Thu, Feb 1, 2018, 12:13 PM

Hi Mrs. Adewumi,

Glad to hear Tanitoluwa is interested in participating.

How much are you able to contribute towards the program?

Thanks,

Coach Russ

I still didn't know whether I was e-mailing a man or a woman, but that was not the biggest problem I was facing. The problem was that question of how much we could contribute. All throughout that afternoon and for much of the next day, I asked myself what the right thing was to do. We had a few dollars left each week from Kayode's job, but that was all. We had some savings, too, though most of the $5,000 that Kayode had brought back with him from Nigeria was gone by this time.

I left it until the next afternoon before I replied.

FROM: Oluwatoyin Adewumi

TO: Impact Coaching Network

DATE: Fri, Feb 2, 2018, 3:33 PM

Good Afternoon sir/ma,

I would love to contribute to this programme, presently we stay in a Shelter, I don't have much with me for now, but my son (TANITOLUWA) is much interested in the chess game.

Kindly assist.

Thank you.

Oluwatoyin Adewumi

Again, Coach Russ replied quickly. And this time . . .

FROM: Impact Coaching Network

TO: Oluwatoyin Adewumi

DATE: Fri, Feb 2, 2018, 6:03 PM

Hi,

Happy to help.

Please register for the program and use the code: fullscholarship

You can find the program listed at impactcoachingnetwork.org

Looking forward to having Tanitoluwa.

Thanks,

Coach Russ

I thought I understood what I was reading, but it was not until I visited the site that it was all clear to me.

I phoned Kayode. I was too excited to explain fully. "They let Tani enroll!"

"Enroll for what?"

"The chess program, they—"

"But we cannot afford it! It is too much for us."

"No, no. Coach Russ—whoever she or he is—has just waived the fee completely. We don't have to pay anything. Tani can start next week."

PART 4
GENEROUS PEOPLE

31 | SO MANY REASONS TO BE HAPPY

OLUWATOYIN ──────────

Sunday mornings in the shelter always began the same way. And the first Sunday in February was no different. Kayode returned from work in time for breakfast, showered, and picked out one of his favorite suits. At 8:00 a.m. we rode the closet-size elevator down to the ground and followed my immaculately dressed husband as he strode out to Park Avenue.

As soon as Tani hit the sidewalk, he exploded into life. He sprinted to the end of the block, head thrown back, arms pumping, his little legs a blur. He has always run like this, fast and free. It's as if he is propelled by his own personal hurricane.

But on this particular Sunday, Tani had two good reasons to be happy. First, the chess program. On Thursday he had attended his first session, and he hadn't stopped repeating the words that Coach Russ—who turned out to be a man—had said at the start:

"In chess, the people who work the hardest are the ones who do the best. Regardless of your circumstances or resources, anyone can be good. All you need is the will and the passion."

Kayode and I both liked the sound of Coach Russ a lot.

Of course, being Tani, he hadn't stopped there. He told us (more than once), "Coach Russ said that one of the best players he has ever worked with grew up in the South Bronx in New York watching YouTube videos. Within less than three years, he went from never playing to becoming one of the youngest American chess masters. Right now he's studying at one of the best universities in the world, and Coach Russ says if he can do it and get so good by being determined and working, there are no excuses for any of us."

So far Tani hadn't asked to borrow my phone to watch chess videos online, but I guessed he'd want to do it eventually. One thing about Tani, he never gives less than 100 percent to anything he's interested in.

Besides the chess program and Coach Russ's words, Tani had another reason to be happy. I had bought him his own chess set and had just given it to him that morning. It cost five dollars, and it was a lot of money, but I figured that I could take it out of that week's food budget, buy less meat, and hope that the boys didn't notice. Seeing the joy on his face as he opened the chess set made Kayode and me happy too.

I always have loved Sundays, but on that Sunday in particular, I knew that we were all blessed. Austin had settled in well at school, and his early grades were excellent, especially in science. Kayode, tired as he was, was looking forward to being away from work until Monday evening. And even though there was a bitterly cold wind blowing down Park Avenue, Austin, Tani, and I were wearing brand-new winter coats—gifts from the kind people at Tani's school.

But mostly, I was happy because we were together. Our little family, so far from home, but united.

Tani stopped when he reached the corner and waited—bouncing on his toes and laughing at the three of us walking with our shoulders hunched against the wind. "Come on!" he yelled. "If you run, you won't feel the cold so much."

When Nigerians dress for church, they don't dress to run. So we walked, and I remembered another reason to be grateful.

I was happy because we were safe. We were in a city filled with millions of strangers from all over the world—a city that knows what it is like to suffer at the hands of terror—and we had nothing to fear. We were safe.

Mom and Dad in 2004. They were both young, but they were going places!

When a prince gets married in Ado Ekiti, he has to look the part!

Mom and Dad's wedding celebration lasted *three whole days*.

My parents' wedding was a blend of African and Western traditions.

Me in Abuja in 2011. My parents say that even as a baby, I was always fascinated by the world around me.

Two happy brothers on a trip to Ado Ekiti to visit family in 2011

Austin and me at home in Abuja. Even back in 2012, our personalities shone through.

Keeping it real on the streets of Abuja, 2014

Our home in Abuja, 2016, not long before our family came to the attention of Boko Haram

Happy and safe—though a little cold!—in the USA

Coach Russ and me sharing a
special moment while crossing
Third Avenue outside of P.S. 116
in Midtown East, New York City

Photo credit: Russell Makofsky

World No. 2 Grandmaster Fabiano
Caruana versus *me* in St. Louis,
Missouri, at a private event during
the 2019 US Championships

Competing at G & T
Saturday quads held at
P.S. 111 in New York City

Me with my first place trophy
after winning the 2019 K–3
New York State Championship
in Saratoga Springs

Photo credit: Russell Makofsky

Coach Shawn and me with my K–3
New York State Championship trophy

Coach Russ celebrating with me
after finding out I clinched the K–3
New York State Championship

Photo credit: Russell Makofsky

Meeting Mr. Nicholas
Kristof from the *New York
Times* in March 2019

Photo credit: Russell Makofsky

Us enjoying a family moment during the taping of *CBS This Morning* with Gayle King

Photo credit: Russell Makofsky

Coach Russ, Coach Shawn, me, and the cast from the *Today* show after appearing on live TV

Photo credit: Russell Makofsky

Playing chess on the set of the *Today* show

Photo credit: Russell Makofsky

Signing our lease on our new home. There were a lot of smiles and prayers of thanks that day.

Photo credit: Russell Makofsky

Coach Shawn and me at the 2019
United States Chess Federation
National Elementary Championship
held in Nashville, Tennessee

Photo credit: Russell Makofsky

P.S. 116 team meeting at the 2019
Elementary Nationals in Nashville

Me at the Elementary Nationals

Rated match play hosted at the 2019
G & T Summer Training Camp held
at P.S. 33 in New York City

Photo credit: Russell Makofsky

Once President Clinton and I started talking about the people we admire, nobody else could get a word in!

My parents with Coach Russ and Coach Shawn. Words cannot express how grateful our family is for these two men.

Photo credit: Russell Makofsky

Coach Shawn, Coach Russ, Coach Angel, and my family outside of the World Chess Hall of Fame in St. Louis, Missouri

Photo credit: Russell Makofsky

Such a lot has changed for our family in recent years. But the love that holds us together remains the same.

The lights turned green when we reached Tani. But when we crossed Twenty-Ninth Street, instead of racing ahead toward the next finish line, he stopped and looked up.

We all followed his gaze.

Tani was looking at a building that had been under construction ever since we moved into the homeless shelter. The work was almost complete, and the safety barriers were finally being peeled away. For the first time we could see the glass and steel beneath. The surface caught the light like a diamond.

"Wow," said Kayode.

We kept walking, but Tani held back, his eyes still locked on the building above. There was something about the way he was looking that made us all stop.

"What is it, Tani?"

He looked back at us, half smiling, half serious. "Very soon," he said, "by God's grace, we will build a very tall building just like that one there. And we will be living on top of it, and all the other floors we will make into a shelter so that other people who need a home can come and live with us."

Kayode straightened his tie, his eyes fixed on Tani. "Amen!" he said, his voice deep and loud and long, like thunder beyond the horizon.

Austin and I joined in too. "A-men! A-men!"

Tani nodded and sprinted off toward the subway, impatient to get to church.

That night, long after we had spent our usual half hour praying, singing, and reading the Bible with the boys before sending them to bed, I lay on my own bed, reading. Kayode was deep asleep on his when suddenly I knew that I needed to go check on the boys.

I rode up in the elevator and saw light coming from under their door. That was unusual. Even before Boko Haram made us a target, the boys had both been excellent sleepers, and nothing about that had changed since moving to America. They always went to sleep as soon as they were told, and they always slept right through till morning. If anything, the challenge was waking them up rather than making them sleep.

I knocked. "Austin? Tani? Are you awake?"

Austin opened the door.

"What's going on?" I said. "Is something wrong?"

Austin looked guilty. He stepped to one side so that I could see what was going on.

He and Tani were obviously in the middle of a game of chess. The board that I had bought Tani was on the floor, in the tiny gap between their two beds. By the looks of it, they had been playing for some time, but the game was nowhere near finished.

I fought to hide my smile and adopted my sternest face instead. "Boys, you should be asleep by now."

"I know," said Tani. "But we're just doing what Coach Russ says."

"And what does Coach Russ say?"

"He says that we should always fight to become better every day. That we should be eager and willing every practice, ready to participate, and hungry to become a better player every day. Please, Mom, it won't take long. Just a few minutes."

I thought for a moment. "Okay. Five minutes. But I'm staying to make sure you finish when you agree."

"Five minutes?" said Tani. "Okay then."

I watched Tani's expression change. He half smiled, half frowned. It was the same look he had earlier when he was looking up at the building and talking about the future. It is a look that I have come to know well over the last two years.

Two minutes and a handful of moves later, Tani slapped down a piece and held out his hand for his older brother to shake.

"Checkmate!" he said, pumping Austin's arm and jumping into bed. "Good night, Mom."

32 | MY FIRST TOURNAMENT

TANI ——————

Austin and I have always been good together. Even when we have the biggest fight ever because he's pulled my covers off in the morning to get me out of bed, and I get so cold that my feet turn to ice, we always, always, always make up within a maximum of two hours. We both like it when everything is good between us.

When I started playing chess, I wanted to tell Austin everything I was learning. I think that some other brothers would not want their little brother doing this—especially when the older brother had tried to teach the little one chess in the first place but basically got it all wrong.

But Austin was good. Austin is *always good*! He wanted me to tell him how to play chess even if it meant telling him that he'd made some mistakes. How great is that?

So I taught him everything that Coach Shawn and Coach Russ taught me. I told him about how the pieces moved, about being in control and making good decisions. I think I got most of it right, and Austin listened hard. Pretty soon we started playing together. And that's when we both started to improve.

When Mom bought me the chess set, we stayed up late *a lot*. Austin didn't even mind that I pretty much always won. He just concentrated hard and stared at the board, and I could tell that he was doing deep thinking even though I had not explained anything about it to him yet.

So I was playing a lot of chess. Even when Austin was not around, I was playing chess using Mom's phone to do chess puzzles at a site that Coach Russ had told Mom about. I liked doing them, and the more I played, the more I wanted to play. I didn't know how many puzzles I was supposed to be doing, so I just kept doing them for as long as Mom would let me have her phone.

I was so excited for Thursday to come around. As soon as school finished at 2:30 p.m., I put on my chess club T-shirt. It's blue and says P.S. 116 NYC on the front, and the letters make chess pieces across the top. It's cool.

When the chess program started at 2:35 p.m., I was at the front. I had already worked out that when Coach Russ and Coach Shawn spoke, I wanted to be able to hear every word and see them up close. They're really different people because Coach Shawn is really soft-spoken and deep thinking and talks like every word is a great chess move. Coach Russ is the opposite. He talks real fast, and his eyes are full of light and life, and even just listening to him talk for a few seconds I start to feel all excited and full of energy.

So when Coach Shawn and Coach Russ both came in and started talking, I was sitting right at the front. They were both explaining about hard work and how important it is to put all your effort in if you want to become good at chess, but some kids behind me were talking, so I turned and shushed them.

I looked back and for a moment thought that I was in trouble. Coach Russ was pointing at me, saying, "I need to talk to you about Tani and Aviel."

I didn't know who Aviel was, but I was so worried. I'd thought that the shush was a good thing, but now I guessed not.

But then Coach Russ smiled at me, and I wondered maybe if I had gotten it wrong. He said, "Now, listen up. You know we keep on telling you how important it is to do your puzzles each week, right?"

Some people said, "Yes, Coach Russ."

"Not all of you are doing them, though, are you?"

Nobody said anything. I wanted to look around but decided not to.

Coach Russ kept talking. "Every time you complete a puzzle on the site, it records it and adds up your weekly total. Coach Shawn and I go through them every week to see who deserves to be celebrated and who needs some more encouragement to work a little harder. And I've got to tell you that last week Aviel and Tani did way more puzzles than anyone else. Some of you did 40, a couple did 50, but Tani did 112, and Aviel did almost 200. That's the kind of hard work and commitment that you need if you want to succeed at this game."

Part of me was really pleased that I had done well. The other part of me was trying to work out how I could beat two hundred next week.

When I went back the next Thursday, I knew exactly what my puzzle number was because I had checked it that morning. I didn't know whether 253 was going to be more than Aviel's, but I didn't mind. The puzzles were cool. Just doing them was fun.

I guess Aviel felt the same way about the puzzles as I did because his total had gone up as well. He was on 283, and the weird thing is that when Coach Russ announced the numbers, I didn't feel bad at all. I just felt happy. I was happy that I had done well and happy that Aviel had done well too.

But what made me feel happier than anything else ever was the conversation I had with Coach Russ at the end of the club. He asked me to come and talk with him by one of the desks, and even though I was kind of nervous as I walked over, I could tell by then that when he smiles, everything is okay. He was smiling.

It was the first time I had actually had a conversation with Coach Russ, and he started by asking me, "What do you like to be called? Tani, or Tanitoluwa like your Mom calls you?"

I said I didn't mind, and he said, "Okay, then, it's just Tani. Now, did you ever play chess before you met Coach Shawn last month?"

I quickly decided not to tell him about the paper chess set. I shook my head and said, "No, Coach Russ."

"And so you've been playing for just three weeks now?"

"Yes, Coach Russ."

He sat back, and his smile got even bigger. "You're working hard and doing really well, Tani. Are you enjoying it?"

I nodded.

Then he said something that made me smile even more than he did. "There's a tournament here on Sunday. Would you like to come and play?"

I didn't know anything much about tournaments or how they worked, but I said, "Yes, please, Coach Russ." I knew that I wanted to be there.

I was so excited when I woke up on Sunday morning. Mom walked with me to school, and it was good that she was there because she got to meet Coach Shawn and Coach Russ. They were all laughing and smiling and talking about things, but I wasn't listening. I was starting to feel like I had eaten something bad and my stomach was complaining about it.

I know now that it was a big tournament. There were 157 players and more tables with chessboards on them than I could count. To me, it was all so big and serious looking. Next to each board was a chess clock. I'd seen them at the club before but hadn't really used one. Coach Shawn must have seen me looking at them because he said, "Don't worry about the clock, Tani. You just hit the button when you've played your move. And if you need help, just ask. We're here."

That made me feel better for a few minutes, but when the tournament started and I sat down to play my first match, I felt worse. I got confused about some of the pieces and drew the first game.

I know that some people think that it's weird to "draw" in a game like chess, but it's really simple. If you can't win and your opponent can't win, then you can offer a draw. You get a half point for it, so in competitions it's better to draw than to lose.

So I drew the first game in the tournament, and I also drew the second game too.

Someone told me that the players I was up against were all beginners just like me, but that didn't help. My head felt hot and my stomach was painful again, and I couldn't stop thinking about how I was not winning. I didn't like it at all.

Coach Shawn sat down next to me while I was waiting for my third and final game. He said, "You know what I think about you, Tani?"

I shook my head.

"I think you're my lion. You're smart, and you're hardworking, and you don't miss a beat. And like a lion cub, you're learning so much right now. Even today, these last two games, you're learning. That's all you need to do. Keep trying. Keep playing. Keep learning. Do your best, remember the openings we talked about, and the winning will take care of itself."

I felt a little better, but not much.

When the last game started, I stopped thinking about winning or losing or drawing and tried to remember the opening that Coach Shawn had told me about. I tried to get my pieces into the center of the board and then protect them with other pieces to make sure they were safe.

It took a long time, and the other player was good and kept on attacking. But he started rushing his moves, and he made a blunder, so I took one of his bishops.

Then I nearly took his queen.

I was getting excited and thinking about how I could figure out another way of taking his queen. He had this knight that was protecting her, and all I had to do was take it. I tried one way, then another. And then he was looking at me, holding out his hand, and saying, "Checkmate!"

I was in tears. Coach Shawn and Coach Russ were saying nice things to me, but I was still in tears. I was standing beside Mom, holding on to her, trying to keep my face away from everyone else.

Coach Russ was saying, "You don't need to feel bad, Tani. You're just three weeks old. Keep on trying. Next one, you will do well."

I didn't want to be rude, but I didn't really want to listen either. I wanted to go back to The Hotel. But Mom was still talking to Coach Russ. She was saying thank you.

Coach Russ said, "He's doing good, Mrs. Adewumi. He's ready to learn, and we can all see that he's a really great guy. We love having him around. This is just the start."

The next Thursday I was back at the chess program. I didn't feel bad anymore, and I had completed more puzzles that week than anyone else. Even Aviel. But I was not so excited about that. There was something else I wanted to find out.

Because I had now taken part in a tournament, my scores were going to be recorded officially, and I would finally have an official rating. Ever since I had joined the program, I had been learning about ratings, and so I knew that the best players in my school were maybe at 1,600 points and that grand masters (the very best players in the world) would have more than 2,500 points.

I found Coach Shawn and asked him about my rating.

He checked his phone and said, "One hundred and five."

Coach Shawn got down on his knees beside me. He said, "You okay with that, my lion?"

I thought for a moment. One hundred and five was low. Really low. It was probably the lowest score you could possibly get. I said, "I think so. I think it means I can improve."

"That's right. You can't get lower. There's only one way you can go now."

33 | WORKING TOWARD THE FUTURE

KAYODE ———————

After four months of washing dishes six nights a week, I was exhausted. I was constantly in pain and feeling as though I were ten years older. I knew that I had to stop.

I was not the only one who felt this way. A lot of the guys at work talked about quitting and making it big one day. They liked talking about their dreams when it was dark outside and there were still hours left to work, but whenever I asked them how they intended to become wealthy, none of them were able to explain their plans in any detail.

I was determined that I would not be trapped in a job that was placing so many demands on my body but giving such little reward. So I decided to find my own route toward success. And I started with Google.

I searched "How do you make it big in America?" There was a lot of different advice, but after careful study, I identified the top three businesses in which people were having the greatest successes. The first was technology. The second was media. I knew that they were both beyond me. I have no training in science or IT, and I lack the capital required to create a media company.

That left the third option, real estate. I had owned property in Nigeria, and I know how to do deals, so I read further. I found out that after a few months of study, I could start out as a real estate agent, work hard, and eventually become a real estate broker, with agents working for me. In time, I could build my own company again.

I knew that was a long way off, and I would need to have saved some money and received my work authorization before I could begin. I also knew that I would need a job that would allow me to study in my free time. Washing dishes just wasn't a good fit for me anymore, so I started looking around for other work.

It was Pastor Phillip who helped again. He introduced me to a woman who owned a domestic cleaning company that worked throughout New York City's five boroughs. The pay was the same as the restaurant, but at least I would be working days instead of nights, and I would not have to do all that heavy lifting and scrubbing.

There was one other significant advantage that made me want to quit the restaurant and take on the cleaning job. My new boss said that if Oluwatoyin was available on the days I was working, she could join me. We would double our income and get to spend time together.

I thought carefully about asking her. She has always been selfless and hardworking, but cleaning people's toilets is not the kind of job you want to introduce to your wife. Besides, Oluwatoyin was already working hard at preparing food for the family and helping the kids with their schoolwork. I was not at all sure that she would want to become a cleaner with her husband.

Yet as soon as I raised the possibility of her joining me, Oluwatoyin agreed. "It's okay," she said. "We just need to survive, don't we?"

Later that week we tackled our first apartment together. It was a great success. I took on the bathrooms while she started working in the kitchen. We talked nonstop, although mainly it was me putting my head around the doorway and telling her, "Hey! Don't forget I am your principal officer. Are you sure you are working hard enough?"

We laughed a lot, worked hard, and were able to clean two different apartments in that one day. We even made fifteen dollars in tips, which was unexpected but very welcome.

Oluwatoyin continued to cook at Pastor Phillip's house on Wednesdays and Fridays, but on most of the other weekdays, she joined me. We fell into a steady rhythm, tackling each new apartment with increasing efficiency. We laughed a lot, but we also were able to talk. We did not discuss the past too often but mainly focused our attention on the present and the future. We agreed that things had been difficult and that we both knew what we needed to do in order to cope.

"I know that I have to pull myself together," said Oluwatoyin. "I might feel down when I am sitting in the room at the shelter, but when I get out, I do not want anyone to see me and think that I am unhappy."

It was helpful for me to hear, and neither of us liked the idea of other people having pity on us. We did not expect anyone to give us money, and we certainly did not want to beg. All we needed was the opportunity to work.

One day when the city was hot and humid, Oluwatoyin and I loaded up our heavy bags of cleaning supplies and took the subway to Brooklyn. It was our first time at the apartment, but I could tell from the name on the contact form that the client was Nigerian. True enough, when he opened the door, he looked just like us.

I introduced myself and Oluwatoyin. He stared. He was clearly confused. "Are you Nigerian?"

Oluwatoyin smiled back. "We are. How long have you been living here?"

He paused, his eyes darting from one of us to the other. "Thirty years," he mumbled. He hung by the doorway, unsure whether to let us in. "Are you sure you want to clean? You don't look like the regular people they send."

"Thank you!" I said. "We've got all our equipment with us and are ready to work. This is what we do."

He stood back and let us in, and we started work. It wasn't unusual for the owner to be in the home while we cleaned, and most of the time, this did not stop Oluwatoyin and me from talking, joking, and laughing. But this man was different. He barely lifted his feet as I swept beneath him, and he sighed as if we were nothing but an inconvenience.

Neither of us felt much like talking.

After we had been cleaning for more than two hours, he pulled from a cupboard five large bags of clothes that looked and smelled as though they had not been washed in months. "I want you to wash all this as well!" he barked.

I had checked the booking carefully before we arrived, as I always did, and there was no mention of doing any laundry. So I held up my hands and tried to explain that my boss had not said anything to us about any laundry.

"I don't care what your boss says. I want you to do my laundry."

"But you did not tell us that we were going to wash clothes. It would have cost another thirty dollars, and we would have started the laundry before we began cleaning. We're nearly finished here, and it would take another three hours to work through what you have there. If you make a booking for next week and say that you want laundry, the boss will make sure there is enough time."

He looked at me as though I were filth. "Get out!" he ordered.

I looked at Oluwatoyin, who seemed as confused as I felt.

"I said get out!" he shouted.

"Okay," I said. "Okay. There is just eighty dollars to pay for the cleaning."

He took a step toward me, his fist clenched. It was obvious he had no intention of paying. "Out!"

He opened the door and we both rushed out, Oluwatoyin still holding her polish and cloth in one hand, me struggling to put on a shoe.

The ride home felt twice as long as the journey there. I was worried that Oluwatoyin was disturbed by the incident. "Were you scared?"

She scrunched up her face and shook her head. "No," she said, smiling and holding my hand. "There is nothing to worry about, Kayode. In fact, I am almost glad for the lesson that it has taught me."

"Really? What lesson?"

"That man was just like some of the people at home. He looked down on us because he thought we were poor, and he took advantage of us because he thought we were weak. Nobody else has treated us this way here in New York. It reminds me that we have been placed right where we need to be—in a city that can give us a future."

"A future of hard work and sweat?"

"Yes! What better future is there?"

34 | MY FIRST *EVER* TROPHY

TANI ————————

It's weird, but do you know that some of the kids who come to the chess program don't really want to play chess? Maybe they like it a little, and maybe they like being with their friends. Maybe they go because there's nobody at home and so they have to stay at school. But they don't love chess.

I don't know how I felt about chess before I played in my first tournament, but after I drew two games and lost one game, something changed for me.

It started with practice. I got *really* into doing the puzzles, and so by the time that I had been playing for one month, I was completing four or five hundred puzzles every week. Then Coach Shawn invited me to enroll in a chess club that he ran every Saturday morning. He said it was in Harlem, so I might not be able to make it, but I asked Mom and she said yes, so I went. It took a long time to get there on the bus, but it was worth it because I got to spend *three hours* playing chess each Saturday.

The other great thing about Saturday chess club was that I got to meet some other kids. *All* of them loved chess, and I liked watching them, especially when I could see that they were doing deep thinking. It doesn't always look the same for everyone, but a lot of people go really still and look at the board like it's about to burst into fire. Some of them stare up at the ceiling as if they are looking for a spider that's hiding in a corner.

The more time I spent playing chess, and the more time I spent around chess players, the more I learned. Of course, I already knew the pieces and how they moved, but what I didn't know was the way that chess is such a big deal in New York.

Coach Shawn was the one who told me the most about it. He told me about people going to Washington Square Park and Union Square Park and other places to play. He said that almost every schoolkid was given an opportunity to learn how to play, and that the city had a special place in the history of the game.

A lot of this was thanks to a man named Bobby Fischer, who some people say was the greatest chess player ever to have lived. His family moved to New York when he was six years old, and they were poor. When they moved, he started to learn chess and played with his older sister, but she got bored, so he had to play on his own. He played a lot and got so good that, when he was thirteen years old, one of the best chess masters in the whole country came to New York to play him. Even though Bobby Fischer was half the age of the master, he won. It was such a famous game that people called it the Game of the Century.

I liked hearing about Bobby Fischer, but I liked it even more when Coach Shawn told me some things about his own life. He said, "Chess saved my life. For a time, I survived by playing blitz on Wall Street for money."

I said, "What's that?"

He said, "Wall Street or blitz?"

I said, "Both."

"Okay, Wall Street is where the really rich guys work in the city. Blitz is when you play but your game only lasts a really short time, like two or three minutes. It's fast, and you've got to be at your best. And if you're playing for money, there are no excuses. It'll cost you if you don't play your best."

Back at The Hotel I discovered that Coach Shawn was right about chess and New York. When some of the people who worked there heard that I was playing, they started inviting me to visit them in the office to play. I liked that, especially when I won.

After I had been playing for two months, I went to another tournament. It was at a different school, and this time there were more tables with boards on them because there were more people who wanted to play. It was louder, and there were lots of people I had never seen before, but I tried not to let my mind be distracted. I just thought about the puzzles I had been doing and remembered how the board looked when I had a really good opening.

Coach Shawn was there, too, of course, and he helped me get ready. There were three or four of us from P.S. 116, and he got us to gather around him in a circle while he said, "You're all my lions. You've all worked hard, and you all can do your best today."

I don't remember much about the tournament. I remember that I won the first game when my opponent made a massive blunder. The second game was tough because I was playing against a boy who was really good and played really fast. It made me get a bit distracted and think about what it would be like to play blitz, but then I told myself to stop thinking about that and concentrate on the game and nothing else. When I did that and made sure I did not think about anything other than the game before me, I won that one too. Then the third game was strange because my opponent kept on looking over at his coach. I think he was nervous, but I just made sure that I controlled the pieces the way I wanted to control them. And I won that one as well.

So I won the tournament!

Everyone was really, really excited for me, and I was sooooooo happy too. People were saying, "Wow! You've only been playing for two months, and you've just gone 3–0!" I liked it when they said that. I liked it when Coach Shawn gave me a massive high five and Coach Russ told me, "I'm so proud of how hard you're working," and when Mom gave me a big hug that lasted forever.

But do you want to know what I liked best about it all?

I won my first *ever* trophy.

The second time I got a trophy, I didn't really win it. It was at a tournament that Coach Russ organized. I finished eleventh, and because it was probably only my sixth or seventh tournament, I didn't know that people who finish eleventh don't usually get trophies. So I was feeling sad when the ten players who finished above me were all invited up at the end to receive theirs.

Just when people were about to leave, Coach Russ came over to me and said, "What's up?"

I told him that I was not happy because I had not won a trophy, and he said, "Wait there."

I waited.

He came back a few minutes later. He was holding a trophy and a pen. I watched him write something on the trophy and hand it over to me. It said:

TANI—MOST IMPROVED PLAYER. NEVER STOP AND NEVER ASK FOR A TROPHY AGAIN.

I looked back at Coach Russ. He was smiling at me.

I decided then that I would never ask for another trophy. If I was going to get any more, I'd win them myself.

Winning my first tournament changed my ranking from 105 to 365, and that made me happy, too, but there were lots of other kids in the chess program who had way higher scores than me. So I just kept doing the same things that I had been doing before. I tried to do as many puzzles as I could each week and asked Austin to play with me whenever he was free. I was always sitting at the front and listening to everything the coaches said at the Thursday chess club, and I did the same on Saturday mornings too.

I said yes to everything that Coach Shawn and Coach Russ suggested. There were different puzzles to try and different openings to learn and there were lots and lots of YouTube videos to watch. And that was how I heard about Fabiano Caruana.

Fabiano is the world number two. He became a grand master when he was fourteen. And guess where he grew up? Brooklyn.

I watched so many videos of Fabiano. He's amazing. He's won almost everything that you can win, and he's really cool.

But this is the best bit. One day, maybe two months after I won my first trophy, Coach Shawn asked me and Aviel and another kid named Lilly to stay behind after club on Thursday.

He said, "There's a charity chess event next week where people pay money to play grand masters. Fabiano is going to be there, and I've been given three tickets to go and watch. Would you three lions like to come along?"

I couldn't speak, I was so excited.

I couldn't sleep much either, especially not the night before.

And on the day of the charity event, when Mom and I showed up and saw Fabiano was *actually there*, I was almost shaking.

It was kind of like a tournament. There were lots of boards laid out and people getting ready to play, but it didn't look much like either of the two tournaments I had been to before. Instead of kids wearing their school chess program T-shirts, there were all these adults wearing suits. And instead of plastic tables and chairs, the tables and chairs here were made of wood, and through the big glass windows you could see almost all of the city.

There were twenty grand masters in the room, and I recognized some of them from the videos I'd watched. They were all smiling and looked really normal, which surprised me because I thought that maybe they would be taller or really serious or kind of different from other people.

But what was even more amazing than seeing all those great chess players was that Coach Shawn told me he was going to introduce me to Fabiano.

I said, "Do you know him?"

And he said, "Sure. He's from Brooklyn, remember?"

And I said, "Do you think he'll talk to me?"

Coach Shawn frowned and looked confused. "Are you kidding? He'd love to."

I followed Coach Shawn as we walked over to a crowd of people. I was really shaking. Everyone looked really tall, and it was strange not knowing anyone because normally at a tournament I would know Coach Russ and Coach Shawn and other coaches as well as some of the players. But here was just a crowd of strangers and I—

Coach Shawn stepped aside, and suddenly Fabiano was standing right in front of me. He held out his hand for me to shake and said, "It's nice to meet you, Tani."

I shook his hand but didn't know what to say. My mouth had forgotten how to speak.

Coach Shawn was smiling and took a photo of Fabiano and me standing together. I was still silent, but I was listening to every word that Coach Shawn said. "You've gotta watch this kid, Fabiano. I'm telling you, he's good. He's been playing four months, and he's already winning tournaments."

35 | ENCOURAGEMENT TO PERSEVERE

OLUWATOYIN ————————

As usual, Tani was full of energy one regular Tuesday morning as we walked to school. It was summer, the long vacation was about to begin, and Tani was excited. The sidewalks were too crowded for Tani to run, but he didn't mind. He skipped along beside me, talking a thousand miles an hour. But it wasn't the prospect of all that time out of school that he was obsessing over. It was something else entirely: a book.

Tani loves to read, and most nights he ends up falling asleep with a book over his face. He reads fast, and as soon as he's finished a book that he likes, he'll talk about it with the same passion and excitement that he shows when he's returned from a great chess session. He talks so clearly and in such detail that sometimes I don't think I even need to read the book myself.

I know where this comes from. My father was passionate about education, and I have always encouraged the boys to read. In New York we started visiting the public library soon after we moved into the shelter, and after an hour or more of sitting quietly and reading, I would encourage the boys to tell me about what they had read on the way home.

The teachers at P.S. 116 were particularly good at introducing Tani to new stories and new writers. In the first few months that we were living in the shelter, Tani told me all about Martin Luther King Jr., President Obama, and Gandhi.

But on this particular Tuesday, Tani was telling me about a nonfiction book he had just finished. I had not heard of the author before, but everything he said about her sounded inspiring.

"This girl lived near the mountains, and she wanted to go to school so badly, but some people said that she should not be allowed to go to school because she was a girl. Instead of doing what they said or staying quiet, she started complaining and telling people that girls should be allowed to go to school. So the bad men shot her."

"And what happened?"

"She survived, but even then, she didn't stay quiet. She kept telling people that girls should be allowed to go to school. Her passion was so great. If not because of her, the girls would not be going to school today. Mom, you need to read the book for yourself."

I told him that I would.

As I walked to the subway to begin my journey to Pastor Phillip's kitchen, Tani's words about my needing to read the book stayed with me. He was right in a way that he couldn't have known. I was struggling a little at the time, and the encouragement to persevere and not give up was just what I needed to hear.

It was the little things that made life hard. Like the fact that you could never have your own key to your room in the shelter. It meant that if you forgot something once you had left the room and closed the door, you had to go up to the seventh floor and wait for someone in the office to become available and escort you back to your room. I spent too many mornings waiting for ten or sometimes fifteen minutes in the lobby while Tani or Austin raced back up to retrieve some homework or other essential item for school that they had forgotten.

The weather was difficult as well. I had guessed that winter in a city this far north would be brutal, but the summer's humidity was something else. There were days when the streets were even worse than the sticky, sweaty heat of Pastor Phillip's kitchen.

Then there was the waiting. Our asylum claim was progressing—or so we were told—but weeks and months crept by and still nothing changed. It was the same with our applications for work authorization and Social Security numbers. All we could do was wait and talk about the next steps we would take as soon as we could officially look for work.

Kayode and I approached the waiting differently. He made a clear and detailed plan that would see him reach his goal of becoming a Realtor. His intention was to save what he could from cleaning houses and then, as soon as the approval was granted, he would buy a car and become an Uber driver and study to become a real estate agent in the evenings.

As much as I could share his excitement and admire his passion and determination, I could not feel the same about my own future. Even though I had a plan of my own to train to become a home health aide, I felt trapped.

I knew why.

Almost as soon as we left Dallas, my uncle started phoning regularly. I was happy enough to talk about how life was for us in New York, but I could tell he wanted more. He wanted to talk about what had happened between us and his wife, to go back and fix things and make sure that it was all neatly resolved. I could not do that. I'd tell him that I was okay, that we were all okay. "We might not be living in the biggest apartment, but I have peace," I said. "I'm not angry with her, but I just don't want to go backward and return to it. If I focus only on the stuff that has happened, I will never move forward. And I need to move forward. I have a lot of things to do. I have to take care of my family. My kids need me."

When we first arrived at the shelter, I'll admit that I was a little nervous. The city was so big and loud and different from anything we had experienced before that I spent too many nights lying awake wondering how things might be about to change. Each day in those first weeks and months seemed to introduce a new danger, a new distraction that was a threat. It wasn't our personal safety that worried me so much—we had made it through Boko Haram, after all. What concerned me was us as a family. Split between two rooms on separate floors, and having lost so much family already, was there a chance that I might be about to lose my boys as well?

But Austin and Tani have always had a strange way of saying or doing the right thing at the right time. Tani's comment about the girl he'd been reading about was typical of him, and it gave me just the right boost of encouragement and optimism that I needed that day. Austin is quieter than Tani, and like his father, Austin won't speak unless he has weighed his words carefully. But so many times when we were in the shelter, he asked me how I was doing or gave me a hug at just the right time. It never failed to go right to my heart.

So I was grateful for them and grateful for my husband, who kept us together and reminded us all of where we came from and where we were going. I was grateful for the friends we had made at church who became family to us and for the people at the shelter, like Miss Maria, who continued to show such kindness every time we saw her. And by the time the summer of 2018 began, and we marked the first anniversary of our arrival in America, there was one other part of our life for which I was now so very grateful.

Chess.

As soon as Tani started at the Thursday after-school chess club and came home repeating Coach Shawn's and Coach Russ's wisdom, Kayode and I knew that the game—and his coaches—had captured his imagination. When Tani started practicing for hours on his own, we knew that this was going to be a major obsession. But it was not until I arrived early to get him from one club meeting and saw the way Tani and the coaches interacted that I understood how deep a connection he was making with them.

Coach Russ and Coach Shawn were standing in front of the board talking about the summer chess camp they were running and why it was a good opportunity for the students to improve. Tani was sitting right in the front row, and he was one of the only kids wearing his blue P.S. 116 chess club T-shirt. "Hey!" said Tani, turning around when a kid at the back started talking. "Listen to Coach Russ. He's serious about all this!"

The coaches smiled at each other. It wasn't as though they were laughing at Tani. Their smiles were warm and full of love. I had the feeling this was not the first time Tani had done it and that they liked it a lot. To see two young men who are proud of your son and love him like you do is one of the greatest gifts a mother can ever receive.

Coach Russ continued, still smiling. "Thanks, Tani, and he's got a point. This matters. If you're coming here and you're not dialed in, you're not going to taste any of the success that you could be capable of. And I look around and I wonder, why is Tani the only one wearing the shirt? And if Tani can do five hundred puzzles each week, why can't you? He's the hardest-working kid here, but he's been playing for less time than all of you."

I watched Tani closely as he listened to Coach Russ. He wasn't turning around to gloat; he didn't seem proud at all. He just looked like he was genuinely glad to be there, and he wanted everyone else to appreciate what they were being taught.

When the meeting ended and Tani went to pack up his bag, Coach Russ and Coach Shawn came to talk to me.

"He's doing so well," said Coach Russ, his eyes sparkling and the words rushing from his mouth. "He's spending twice as much time practicing as the most engaged kids in the program. They do two hours each day, and he does four. And like you've seen, he's right there at the front, his hand up first, always focused, always listening. We've got other kids in the program with the same rating, but Tani's intensity and maturity are way higher than most. He's a great kid."

"Thank you, Coach Russ. You are both so kind to him."

"Are you kidding?" said Coach Russ. "Tani's great, and we love having him on the team. It's Coach Shawn who's really working closely with him."

Coach Shawn was different. He moved more slowly, with precision and purpose. But there was the same smile on his face when he talked about my son. "Tani's like a nephew to me. He's mature for his age, he listens so well, and he always takes things in, even the life lessons that I try and teach them. When he plays, he's always looking to win. He's like a tiger with feelings."

Tani came over, grinning at the three of us.

"What do you think about summer camp, Tani?" said Coach Russ. "Could you join us?"

"Yes, please, Coach Russ."

I shifted a little, and Coach Russ must have noticed because he said, "We have money set aside for Tani's place. It's all taken care of, if he'd like to come. And if Austin wants to come along and earn some money by helping out, we'd be happy to have him too."

I didn't know what to say.

"Mrs. Adewumi, this isn't charity. My priority is building winning chess programs and developing strong players, and Tani's skill and attitude are impressive. If Tani wasn't so passionate with such tremendous raw talent, I wouldn't be pushing him so hard, but he has it all, and I want him around our program. His excitement is infectious, and he makes the others want to work harder. And this isn't the first time we've done this, and we've found that sometimes our best kids are the ones who take advantage of these opportunities that we give them because they don't have so many opportunities in life. So what do you say? Can he come? We'll take good care of him."

I still wasn't sure what to say. There was never any doubt in my mind about whether they would keep Tani safe. Everything I had seen so far had told me that the coaches were good people who were offering a great service. What was holding me back was the fact that I didn't know how to say a big enough thank-you for all they had done. It wasn't just the scholarship or the life lessons they were teaching Tani. It was more than that. They were giving Tani the one thing that was impossible for Kayode and me to provide, no matter how hard we worked. They were giving him the opportunity to belong to a wider family.

"Yes," I said. "I would never trust anyone with my children, but I trust you with him."

36 | BECOMING A STUDENT OF THE GAME

TANI ————————

$$45 - 1 = 44$$

That's the number of days I went to summer camp last summer.

$$44 \times 8 = 352$$

We spent 8 hours a day playing chess or talking about chess or just doing things that helped us get better at chess. So that means I spent 352 hours practicing chess at camp.

$$1{,}100 - 550 = 550$$

At the start of the camp, my rating was 550. At the end it was 1,100. That means it doubled in two months.

$$550 \div 352 = 1.56$$

So for every hour I was at camp, my rating improved by more than one and a half points.

Camp was great. I'd never been to a summer camp before. In Dallas, when school was out, we just stayed at Grandma's house and tried to keep quiet and not leave the bedroom, and I don't think we had camp in Nigeria in the summers.

There were two things I liked a lot about camp. First were all the people who were there. Even though most of them were my age, some of them were really, really good at chess. They came from all over the country, not just Manhattan, and some had ratings as high as 1,600 and were state champions. I think that one of them was even number two or three in the whole country for their age group. And because they were all really nice, they let me play them. I didn't get to beat too many of them, but there were some games when I could tell that they were having to think really, really deep to beat me.

It wasn't just the other kids that made me like being there. As well as Coach Russ and Coach Shawn, other coaches were there too. I liked them all, especially Coach Angel. He moves slow and his voice is really gentle, but he's one of the nicest people I've ever met. I think that's why Coach Shawn says they are such good friends and that "Brothers couldn't be closer."

The other thing I liked about camp was the fact that Coach Russ organized it and invited Austin to come and help out. That meant that he and I could take the subway together, which was fun. Also, Austin started playing chess properly, and he started to get good too.

One day Coach Russ said, "Today we're going to be playing bughouse. Tani and Austin, do you want to go together?"

I was really happy and said, "Yes, please, Coach Russ!" but Austin was confused and said to me, "What's that?"

I said, "Bughouse is so cool. You and your partner play as a team against other pairs. You sit next to each other and both play your games at the same time, but any time you capture one of your opponent's pieces, you give it to your partner, who can then put it on their board and use it."

When you play bughouse, you're allowed to give your partner advice, but it didn't take Austin long to work it out. And then *bam*! We won our first game really quickly. Then we won the next game and the next, and when we were 5–0, we won the whole tournament! There wasn't a trophy, but that was okay. Austin was smiling so big that he didn't even tell me to stop when I was doing the floss dance super fast to celebrate.

All through the summer I didn't know that my rating was going up, but I knew I was getting better. I was really trying hard to do deep thinking, and even though it wasn't really easy, it wasn't as hard as it used to be. If I concentrated and wasn't too tired, I could think three or four moves ahead. The longer camp went on, the closer I got to beating some of the best kids there.

Right at the very end of camp, Coach Russ and Coach Shawn invited me to go on a trip somewhere called the Hamptons. I had to get up really early and say goodbye to Mom at Penn Station and then sit on a train for a long, long time, but it was worth it.

It was like a one-day summer camp where everyone talked about and learned about chess. It was in a school, too, but the thing that I remember the most about it was that I got to play a boy who was just one year older than me but had been playing for a long time and had a rating that was higher than 1,300.

When the game was over, Coach Shawn asked me to sit down with him.

He said, "Tani, what do you think about that game?"

I said, "Well, I won, so that was good. Wasn't it, Coach Shawn?"

He shook his head. "No, you didn't just win, Tani. You destroyed him. You were tactical, you played aggressively, you were smart and controlled and disciplined. That was . . . I don't know what it was, but I was sitting there watching, and I just kept on saying to myself, 'Wow!'"

There wasn't much more to do for the rest of the day, so Coach Shawn and I played a game. He's a chess master with a rating of something like 2,200, so he won, but I was watching him, and there were some moments in our game when his face went really still and his eyes stared really hard at the board, so I think he was having to concentrate.

After we finished playing, I set up the board again and said, "Coach Shawn, I want to show you something."

He said okay, and I started playing both the white and the black pieces.

White pawn to E4.

Black pawn, E5.

White knight, F3.

Black knight, C6.

I knew exactly which piece I wanted to move and where I wanted it to be, and as I played, I was happy because the patterns on the board were right. I wasn't doing deep thinking because I already knew how the game was going to end, but I liked it anyway.

I made white sacrifice a pawn but get nothing for it. Then white and black traded a pawn each. Then they traded another pawn each.

Then Coach Shawn said, "I know this game!"

I didn't say anything back because I was too busy concentrating and just about to make white sacrifice a pawn, a bishop, and a knight and only get a bishop in return.

"That's right," said Coach Shawn. "You remember what comes next?"

I nodded and played on. Black was looking strong, but white was clever. White had laid a trap by sacrificing all those pieces, and black's king was exposed and weak. A few moves later, and it was over. White had won.

Coach Shawn gave me a fist bump and said, "Paul Morphy, huh?"

I nodded.

If you don't play chess, you probably have never heard of Paul Morphy. But if you do play chess, then you will *definitely* have heard of him because Paul Morphy was one of the greatest chess players ever. He was the first unofficial world champion, and as soon as I'd heard some of the coaches talking about him during summer camp, I liked him.

Paul Morphy was from a place called New Orleans, and he lived so long ago that there was no such thing as electricity, and there were probably still slaves near where he lived. His dad played in the kitchen every Sunday, and Paul Morphy would watch him.

One day, when he was eight years old, he said to his dad, "Can I play you?"

His dad said, "I've never taught you how to play. How can you play me?" He really wanted to play, and his dad said yes, and they played. And Paul Morphy won.

His dad was really impressed and took him to his chess club. He won there too. And the more he played the better he got, and he got so good that he became one of the best players in the whole world. He might even have been *the* actual best player, but this was such a long time ago that the official organization of chess hadn't even been set up, so there was nobody organizing world championship matches. But if there had been, and Paul Morphy had played, he probably would have won.

Coach Shawn had told me about Paul Morphy and how most other players at the time played really slowly, but Paul Morphy was totally different and played really fast and aggressively and won games in as little as twenty moves. That's quick.

Even though Paul Morphy was alive a long time ago, he still did what every chess player does today, recording the moves he made in each match in a little book. So today there are hundreds of his games that you can look up online, and you can see for yourself how great a player he was.

All through that summer I looked up his games whenever I could. I liked the way he laid traps and controlled the center of the board and was willing to sacrifice pieces so that he could win. One of my favorite games is from when he was in Paris, France, playing against two men who were helping each other. It's called the Opera Game because they were at the opera house, and there was an actual show going on, but they were playing chess instead. Maybe his opponents were distracted by the singing, but I don't think so. Paul Morphy even sacrificed his queen just so he could win. It's a great game, and you should definitely look it up.

I liked the Opera Game a lot, but that wasn't the one that I showed Coach Shawn that day when we were in the Hamptons. The one I showed him was one of the first games Paul Morphy played against his dad. I think that he was only ten or eleven years old at the time, and maybe he'd only been playing a few years. That's why I liked it.

When I'd finished playing and was packing away the board, Coach Shawn said, "That's the thing about chess, Tani. If you keep playing well and start to become well-known as a player, your opponents will study up on you before you meet. There's no more hiding your style."

I knew the games of great players like Paul Morphy and Bobby Fischer and Fabiano and all the others were available, and I liked looking at them online. But I'd never thought about looking up an opponent's matches. And I'd never thought that anyone would look up mine. So I thought about what Coach Shawn said for a while and then said, "So I need to get really good at memorizing lots of different games?"

"Kind of," said Coach Shawn. "But it's not really about just memory. If someone has studied you and you always play the same moves, then they know what you're going to do. If you're predictable then you're vulnerable. They might set traps or change the style of the game so that it makes it really hard for you to play the kind of game that you want to play."

That didn't sound good at all. I liked winning, and most of the time I did it by playing the way I wanted to play. I didn't like the idea of people not letting me play that way.

Coach Shawn was smiling. "It works to your advantage too. If you can craft your game around the fact that someone may be looking up your public matches and following you, move by move, you can turn that to your advantage. You can lay traps, and you can lead them where you want to."

"Like Paul Morphy?" I asked.

"Exactly!" said Coach Shawn. "You don't just win by playing the board. You've got to get in their heads as well."

37 | DRESSED WITH DIGNITY

KAYODE ──────────

Thirty.

That is the number of suits I brought with me from Nigeria. I understand that thirty is a lot of suits for anyone to bring with him when he moves from one country to another, especially an asylum seeker who lives in a homeless shelter. But I have always believed that the way in which you present yourself will have an impact on how people respond to you. If you take no care in your appearance, then surely people will assume that you do not see yourself as being worthy of care. If it is obvious from just one look that you do not believe in yourself, then why should anyone else?

The whole four months that I worked in the restaurant kitchen and then for the seven months I spent cleaning people's homes, I had to dress for the job. I had to wear tennis shoes and T-shirts and jeans. In other words, I had to dress nothing like a man who believes he is going somewhere in life. I had to dress like someone who was lost.

Don't get me wrong: I do not dress to make people believe I am special and above others. I am not an arrogant man, and I do not need people to love me. But I do want to be treated with respect and to have people treat me with dignity. Why is that? Not because I am a prince or the grandson of a king. Not because I have owned a business and property and achieved some of my goals in life. I want to be treated right because of the simple truth that I am a human being just like you, and we all have dignity. We all deserve to be treated well.

So all those months that I worked for six dollars an hour were difficult for me. I felt invisible and overlooked. More than anything, I felt as if I had to forget about a part of me, the part that I had inherited from my father and grandfather, the part that people would look to for help, for advice, for support.

Of course, I had no other choice than to put those feelings aside and keep working. My suits remained jammed in my closet, packed in bags under the bed, or hanging on the back of the door. Only once each week, on Sunday, could I pull one out and return to my old, familiar self.

But all of this changed when Oluwatoyin and I received our Social Security numbers and work authorizations. From that point on I was no longer one of the million-strong army of unofficial workers in the city. I was finally able to put my plan into action and take the next step toward making it big.

It was not quick, and there were more tests to take and forms to fill out and hurdles to be cleared, but as our one-year anniversary of being in the shelter approached, I finally became an Uber driver.

It changed things for us as a family. Even though I was paying for gas as well as $350 each week to rent a car (another Toyota Camry, just like my car back in Nigeria), I was able to earn more money than I had from either of my previous two jobs. If the boys needed sneakers or Oluwatoyin needed clothes, we could finally afford it.

Having the car also saved us time. I was able to take Oluwatoyin to and from Pastor Phillip's house when she went there to cook, and on Sunday mornings we no longer had to wake up at seven in the morning and spend two and a quarter hours on two trains and a bus in order to get to church. We could simply leave the shelter at 9:30 a.m. and arrive feeling well.

I started work each day at 6:00 a.m. and finished at 6:00 p.m., just in time to make it to the real estate class I had enrolled in on Sixth Avenue.

If I had time between jobs during the day, I would park and study, but I was careful not to neglect my duties as an Uber driver. I was committed to making it a success, and even before I started the job, I knew exactly how I would do that. I offered all my passengers a complimentary bottle of water and had a full range of cell phone adapters plugged in and ready to charge whatever device they used. If they coughed, I offered them tissues and more water, and I always opened the door for them at the start and end of each journey.

And, of course, I always, always wore a suit.

It did not take long for people to notice. Some of my passengers would ask how long I had been driving, and they would often be surprised when I told them it was only a matter of weeks or months. Others said they liked how clean and well equipped the Camry was. But nearly all of them commented on my suits. They'd tell me I was sharply dressed, and I'd tell them about my father in Nigeria, who was the son of a king, and how he would always tell me, "Son, how you dress is how you will be addressed." My passengers often liked hearing that story, and I liked telling it.

I liked it even more when I got home at the end of the day, checked the app, and saw the tips that I had earned.

The biggest change of all was how it made me feel.

When someone sees you the same way that you believe you can be seen, it is such a powerful thing. Nobody ever questioned why I was cleaning pans in the restaurant, and only occasionally when I was cleaning houses did someone say, "Hey, you're well dressed there" or "You're doing a good job." But Uber was different. Uber gave me the opportunity for people to look at me in a new way.

In many ways there is nothing different about washing pans or cleaning apartments or driving people from one meeting to another. You are still serving people by performing a task they do not wish to perform themselves. But by keeping my car immaculate, telling my stories, and wearing my suits, I was no longer invisible to most people. I was able to be myself again.

For months I had been working hard in the hope that it would pay off and that one day I would see the rewards. Between Uber and my evenings spent studying to become a real estate agent, I regained so much of my old confidence. I would sit in the class on Sixth Avenue tired from twelve hours of driving but eager to learn and excited about the doorway that would open once I passed.

Of course, it was not easy. But I had a lifetime of lessons in perseverance to draw on. Every time someone stood up at the front and told us how lucky we would be to pass or how difficult it was to make it in real estate, I had so many memories to draw on. Working on a building site for my father in the heat of the African sun, hauling paper and ink around the printshop, struggling with scalding water and thick layers of grease in the kitchen while my family was asleep at home. I am not a lazy man. I know that hard work pays off.

One evening when the course was nearly over, I listened to a broker who stood at the front and told the room that only those of us who were fortunate would pass the test. I waited in line at the end, introduced myself, and asked him for a card.

One month later, just minutes after I had received the e-mail notifying me of my passing the test, I dialed his number.

"Good morning, sir," I began. "My name is Kayode Adewumi, and I am one of the fortunate ones."

38 | TAKING TIME TO THINK

OLUWATOYIN ─────

I said goodbye, watched Tani run into school, and paused. Tani had been particularly talkative that morning, his eyes wide, full of excitement as we walked. His joy had nothing to do with the first fall of snow on the ground or the fact that Christmas was less than a month away. Coach Russ had invited and paid for him to attend a tournament in Orlando, and we were due to leave in two days.

My phone buzzed in my pocket. A text from Grandma was the last thing I was expecting. As I opened the message, I could feel my pulse rise.

By the time I'd finished reading it I was almost ready to faint.

"You know that your uncle is sick. He's got worse and had some tests. The results are bad. He has one month to live. Call me."

I did what she said. I spoke with Grandma. Our call did not last long. It was our first conversation since we had left Dallas, and she sounded older, like the one year that had passed since she asked us to leave had really been ten. She told me that he had cancer and that the hospital had said there was nothing more they could do for him.

"How is he?"

Grandma started to say something then stopped herself. "Dying," she said quietly. "But peaceful."

Another pause.

"You can come visit him if you want, Oluwatoyin."

"Thank you," I said.

Our words dried up, and there was nothing else to say.

I spoke to my uncle as soon as I could, but though he said he was happy for me to visit, he did not want to talk too much on the phone. He said it made him tired, and I could hear the energy draining from his voice minute by minute. He passed the phone back to Grandma, and we fixed a date for me to visit soon after Tani and I returned from the tournament, and we said goodbye.

As soon as we arrived in Orlando, I was aware that part of my head and heart were in Dallas. I wanted to support Tani and the coaches and be there to celebrate the team, but I also wanted to be with my uncle. The news of him dying was like an instant wound had opened up in my flesh. There was a constant ache, a pain that sometimes retreated into the background a little but could never be completely forgotten. At any particular moment, without any warning at all, the sadness and the fear and the shock could come screaming back into me. I was torn in two, and it hurt more than I imagined.

"How are you managing it?"

I looked up and saw a mom that I knew from New York. I was sitting on the floor in the hotel corridor while Tani was playing a match in the meeting room nearby. Parents and coaches aren't allowed in the room when tournament matches are being played, and most of the time we hang out together in a team room with Coach Russ, Coach Shawn, the other coaches, and the all the parents with kids in Coach Russ's programs. Most of the time I like it in there. I sit and talk and join in the laughter with everyone else. But on the first morning in Orlando, I found myself drifting along the corridors, happy to be quiet and on my own.

This mom, Tori, sat down and smiled. "Your son, Tani, he's so passionate about the game. My boy's always talking about him. How do you get him to stay so engaged like that? Do you have to keep on at him to practice? Is it as hard for you as it is for me?"

"Thank you," I said. "You're very kind." I wondered if she had any experience of what it was like to live in a homeless shelter, but looking at the way she was dressed, I guessed not. So I decided not to tell her about that part of our lives. Instead I told her what any mom would understand. "When he comes home from school or Thursday practice, he eats, then he takes a nap. I wake him up at maybe six thirty or seven, and he does his homework and eats some more if he's still hungry. After that he can do whatever chess things his coaches have set for him, then play puzzles or play with his brother until nine. Then we pray until nine thirty, then bed."

"You're lucky," said Tori. "I come back from work so late, and I don't have time to help him. But I want him to do well here. This is such a great opportunity, don't you think?"

"That's true," I said. "Chess is such a good thing in Tani's life. In all our lives."

We sat for a moment and both watched the crowd as it flowed past us. I'd been to tournaments with Tani before, but they were always local. They were mostly held in schools and lasted a single day. But the one in Orlando was way bigger than anything I had seen before, as kids from all over the US gathered to compete. The competition was spread over three days, there were hundreds of children ready to play, and the whole place was full of noise, crowds, and excitement.

A team-room door next to us opened, and a boy not much older than Tani burst out, followed by a man I guessed was his father.

The dad looked mad, his face red and neck veins bulging. "You drew?" He shouted, loud enough to make other people stop in the corridor and look. "Why'd you have to draw?"

The kid threw his chessboard down on the ground. "Why are you always on at me like this? What will you do if I lose?"

The father glanced around and must have seen people looking at him. He leaned in and whispered something. The boy's face turned red. He started crying. "I'm not playing anymore!"

This was the first time I'd seen anything like this. Most of the time, parents were encouraging and supportive, especially in the team room with Coach Russ, Coach Shawn, and all the others. There are always a lot of hugs and high fives, fist bumps and laughter whenever they're around. And after every match the players bring out their notation books, in which they have recorded the match move by move, and the coaches huddle round and analyze them. It's a special time, and the conversations are full of praise and encouragement. And where they find a mistake, the coaches seem to have an ability to help the players see it for themselves and work out what else they could have done.

Tori went to get a snack, and I drifted back to our team room to be ready for Tani when he finished his match. It was quiet in the room, with just a handful of parents sitting around chatting quietly or reading.

Coach Russ came over to me and asked how I was. I hadn't told anyone about my uncle, and I did not know how. Besides, being in Orlando was a good distraction. So I didn't have to lie when I told him that I was well and happy to be at the tournament.

"Tani was pretty excited this morning, huh, Mrs. Adewumi?"

"Very excited! He's been talking about this ever since you invited him. It was so kind of you to make it possible for us to come."

He waved his hands. "Don't mention it. It's all taken care of. And you know, we just love having Tani around. Everybody loves him. He's a special kid."

"Thank you, Coach Russ."

Coach Russ paused awhile. "You know, this tournament is a big step up for him. He's always asking me, 'Am I doing good? Am I working hard enough? Am I number one?' The answer is often yes back home, but here it's going to be different. Here he's up against kids who've been coached for years. Kids from families with no limit to their resources. Kids who spend their whole year traveling around the country to attend events like this. So the question isn't whether he's going to win a trophy, because, barring a miracle, he's really not. The question I'm fascinated by is, how is he going to respond to coming such a long way back from the winners? You remember that tournament with the trophy, don't you?"

I did. "He's still got that trophy in his room, Coach Russ."

"That's good. And I want him to get a whole lot more as well. But he's got to be hungry enough for them that he fights for them on the chessboard, that he dedicates himself to getting better every day. Don't get me wrong—he has a lot of heart. He works hard, doesn't fear the challenge, and he's got talent. But there are a ton of other kids like that here today. The difference between them and the champions is how they handle the pressure. Can they keep their mind-set correct all through the tournament and not get distracted, even when there's so much going on around them here? That's our job as coaches, to figure out what is going on with the games and help keep his mind-set correct."

There was movement on the other side of the room, and the door from the match hall opened. It was Tani. He looked at me and then at Coach Russ and held out a fist with the thumb stuck up. A first-round victory.

But Tani wasn't happy. He wasn't bouncing like he had been before, and after giving me a quick hug, he walked over to Coach Shawn, pulled open his notation book, and got to work.

The more I listened to them talk, the warmer I felt inside.

"Look at this, Tani, knight to G3. This is what I'm talking about. You make moves of such quality. They're so confident and bold."

"Yeah, but I blundered. I could have lost."

"True, but you didn't lose, and you know where you blundered, don't you?"

"That move," he said, pointing to the book. "I left myself exposed."

"That's right. You blundered, but you saw it. And let's make it a positive and ask, what did you learn from this?"

Tani thought for a moment. "I need to not rush."

"There you go. That's a lesson right there. And it's a lesson that can take years to learn fully. But today you've got a jump on the other guys who haven't even started to figure it out."

Tani sighed. "But I've got six more rounds to go. What if I blunder again?"

"You just take it one round at a time. Let's not focus on a prize. Let's focus on the work, okay?"

"Yes, Coach Shawn."

"All right. So you've got a couple of hours before your next game, and I want you to look at your openings and do another twenty puzzles. That okay? Good. I want you to keep calm, keep your mind engaged on the game, and don't allow yourself to get distracted. Can you do that, Tani?"

"Yes, Coach Shawn."

By the time his next round of matches was about to start, Tani was bouncing with excitement again. Coach Shawn pulled all the players from P.S. 116 together and told them to listen up.

"To be a champion you have to have the mind-set of a champion. Remember what Magnus Carlsen said when the journalist asked him if he was going to win the tournament?"

All five players answered as one, chanting the words together. "I'm not worried about winning, I'm worried about playing my best."

"That's right. Now, I've got something for you all." He dug around in his backpack and pulled out a handful of chess pieces. It was only when he had handed his players one each and they held them up that I could see they were all the same.

"You're the Knights of the Round Table, remember? I watched you all these last two hours, and you've all been working so hard. You've been focused and calm, and I know for sure that right now you're ready to go into battle. You're ready to do your absolute best."

Tani and the other four hadn't taken their eyes off Coach Shawn since he'd called them over. He was like a magician performing a trick or an artist creating a beautiful picture right in front of their eyes. They were completely under his spell.

"Now," said Coach Shawn, checking the time, "we're ready to go. Who's feeling confident?"

Five hands shot up into the air.

"That's good, that's good. So let's bring up the confidence meter."

They all put their hands in the middle, low at first, then bringing them up as one, cheering and laughing the higher they went.

"Okay, okay, last thing now. We got to build each of you up before we send you into battle in there. Who wants in first? Tani? Okay, come right in here. What do we say everyone?"

"Taa-ni! Taa-ni! Taa-ni!"

The chanting grew louder and louder until it was a shout that filled the room. By the time the door to the match hall opened, Tani and the other four players from P.S. 116 almost ran in.

I didn't leave the team room for much of the rest of the day. I liked being there. It was quieter than it was out in the corridor, and it was good to be able to talk to the other parents. And the way that the coaches and the other parents talked to me left me feeling like I was part of the team too.

It was only when Tani went for his fourth and final match of the day that I left the room. All day I'd seen other parents offer to buy the coaches coffee or share their food with them, and I'd seen a market on the way into the hotel the day before.

"Mrs. Adewumi," said Coach Shawn when I returned and brought him a plate of roast chicken, rice, and plantain. "This is too kind of you. I can't."

I fixed him my best Nigerian Mama stare. "Coach Shawn, I'm so grateful to you for all you're doing for my son. Please, accept this gift from me to you."

He smiled and leaned his face over the plate. "Well, it does smell pretty good. But can I pay? Please, let me give you something for this."

This time I didn't just give him the Nigerian Mama stare. I folded my arms and raised my eyes.

"Okay, okay. I'm not going to win here, am I?"

"No, you're not, Coach Shawn. Know when you're beaten. Now, please, eat up."

39 | GIFTS BEFORE CHRISTMAS

I won my last game at the tournament in Orlando and ended up with three wins, one draw, and three losses. I was in ninety-fourth place. It wasn't as high as some of the people that came from New York, but it was okay for me, I guess. Coach Russ and Coach Shawn both told me that it was a good score to get because I hadn't been to a big tournament like that before, and there was a lot to learn about it.

They were right. Every other tournament I'd played in had seemed big, but this one was really big. The match hall was noisy, and there were lots of people everywhere you looked, so it was easy to get distracted. And some of the people I played were really good and played really fast and really confidently. All those things added together meant that I was not playing at my best.

There was one more big difference, but not the kind of difference that affected my score. At this tournament there was even a shop. Not a shop selling food snacks but a shop selling things that would help you play chess—such as books and boards and all kinds of great stuff. I'd seen it on the first morning, and all through the tournament I'd heard people talk about what they were going to buy and how much money their moms or dads had given them.

I didn't have any money of my own, and I didn't want to ask Mom. So I kept quiet and waited until someone started talking about something else.

When the tournament was almost all over and we were sitting around the team room, waiting for the last games to finish, I saw people walking around the room with bags from the shop. Some of my friends came over to me and showed me what they'd bought. "Hey, Tani," they'd say. "Look at this cool clock I got. It's digital and the lights are all different colors." Or, "Hey, Tani, I got this book—d'you wanna see it?"

I definitely liked everything they'd bought. But I definitely also felt like I really didn't want to look too long at the clocks or books or whatever, because if I did, then I started to feel weird inside.

Coach Shawn had been sitting with me, but he left when everyone started coming over to show me their things. I wondered whether maybe he didn't have much money either.

But then I saw him coming back into the team room. He had a bag just like everyone else, and so I knew that he'd been to the shop too.

He said, "Hey, Tani. Come here, will you?"

I went over to the corner of the room where he was standing. He said, "I got an early Christmas gift for you." He was holding open the bag so I could see inside.

It was a chess bag. But it wasn't just a regular chess bag. It was the best chess bag I'd ever seen in my *entire life*. It was black and made of leather and had a shoulder strap as well as two handles, and it had a rolled-up board inside and all the pieces as well as space for a clock and a notation book and pens. It was amazing and the best present I'd ever been given, ever.

I jumped up on a chair and gave Coach Shawn a hug. I didn't want to let go, but I did let go because I wanted to check my bag out some more.

Coach Angel came over and said, "What's that, Tani?" And I showed him the bag, and he was impressed too. Then Mom came over and she liked it, and I put it on my back and tried walking around with it. Everyone was like, "Tani! Great bag!" or "Tani, you look so professional!" And I was grinning so much my face was almost hurting.

Then Coach Angel came back, and he said, "You can't have a great bag like that and not have a clock. Here. Merry Christmas!" And he gave me this amazing digital clock that fit perfectly in my bag. And then another coach who I didn't even know as well as Coach Shawn or Coach Angel came over and gave me a new notation book that he'd just bought for me from the shop too. I was laughing and saying thank you and laughing some more. Mom was laughing, too, but she was crying as well because that's the kind of thing moms do at times like this.

I kept the bag on all the way back to my room. And then at the airport the next day when someone asked if I wanted to check the bag, I said, "No way! I'd like to keep it, please, sir," and I did. I wore the bag all the way back to New York.

Even when we landed and got outside the airport and were waiting for Dad to come pick us up, I was holding the bag. Coach Shawn was telling Mom that he was going to get an Uber, but Mom told him, "No, Coach Shawn, my husband will drive you."

"But Tani's got school tomorrow, and it's late already." Coach Shawn was trying really hard to persuade Mom to let him go, but Mom wasn't stopping. She had her arms folded and was lifting her eyebrows up really high.

"Coach Shawn," I said. "You don't want to argue with my mom when she's looking at you like that. Just apologize and do whatever she says quickly. That's what my brother and I do."

PART 5
BLESSED

40 | SEASONS CHANGE

OLUWATOYIN ————————

On January 29, Grandma phoned to tell me that my uncle had died. I'd made a trip to Dallas just after Christmas and said my goodbyes to him in the hospital, but the news still felt like a shock. Two months earlier I'd thought he was just as healthy as ever. And now he was dead.

Grandma phoned me a couple of times in the days after he passed. She said she wanted to find out more about him, and she listened as I told her everything I knew about his life in Nigeria. She was softer, kinder. Even though I hated the reason, I liked the change in her.

And then—silence. For several days I heard nothing from her. When I did finally call her, and I asked about the funeral, she said, "We're burying him tomorrow. Four in the afternoon. Can you come?"

I wanted to ask her why I was only finding out about the funeral now, a day before. I wanted to know what she was thinking and why she was still playing games at a time like this. But I didn't have the energy. I told her I'd talk with Kayode and let her know.

In the end, I didn't go. It was obvious that she didn't want me there, and I figured that if I showed up, she would find another way of reminding me that I was not a part of her family.

I believe that there are seasons for grieving and seasons for living, and the change from one to the other can be as quick as an African sunrise. For me, it was just a few weeks after my uncle's death that I noticed the swift transition.

It was a regular Thursday afternoon, and I walked to P.S. 116 to get Tani from his chess club. Coach Russ was there, and after we'd talked a little, it was clear that he had something he wanted to say. He's always full of energy, his eyes smiling bright, but this time he was even more excited.

"In a few weeks it's the state championship in Saratoga Springs, and Tani's rating is high enough for him to qualify. I'd love for him to be there. A lot of people are going to be there, and Tani will have to play six games over two days against some of the best players in New York State. It's not going to be easy, but it will be a great experience for him. What do you say?"

Tani had been hanging on every word his coach had said, and he barely paused for breath before he said, "Yes, please, Coach Russ."

Both of them turned to look at me.

"What do you think, Mrs. Adewumi? Would you come too? It's a long drive, and there will be a lot of waiting around, and we won't be staying in a hotel, but we'd love to have you with us."

I could feel the season shifting from grieving to living again. So I smiled. "I will be very happy to come with you too, Coach Russ."

41 | ON TO THE STATE CHAMPIONSHIP

TANI ———————

One day while we were walking to the basketball court, Austin and I talked about Mom and Dad.

I said, "What do you most like about them?"

Austin started talking about Dad and said, "He's hardworking and wants the best for us, and he's always reminding us to focus and pay attention and become a great person in life."

I said, "I like all those things too."

Then Austin said, "Wait, I forgot. I have one more thing to add about Dad. I like his suits."

That was funny, but not in a rude way, because Dad really does have a lot of suits, and all of them look really good.

Then I said, "What about Mom?"

Austin thought for a moment. He said, "She's the best at teaching moral lessons, and she's always trying to guide us away from bad things. Did you know the other day when I was on a school trip, some kids were messing around badly, but I made them stop because I remembered all those stories she'd told us about how important school is?"

(Austin had already told me that story about the school trip, but I nodded anyway.)

We reached the court then, and it was time to play, so *I* didn't get to say what I like most about Mom. But all the time we were playing I was thinking about her and what my answer would be.

I like that she cooks good food. She can make anything taste good, and all the time we were living at The Hotel, I think she really missed not having a kitchen of her own.

I like that she corrects me. Well, maybe I don't like it, but I know that it's helpful, so I'm grateful for that.

Most of all, I like that she helps me in my chess. When I don't play well, she doesn't get mad or make a big deal out of it like some parents do. She just says, "Do you think you can do better?" And I say yes, and she says, "Well, if you work hard and concentrate and do your very best, that will be good enough." And she takes me to chess tournaments. She's never too busy even though she also takes Austin to his basketball games and cooks all the time and has her own job too.

So my mom is good at sharing her time with us, and my dad works harder than anyone else I know and will do anything to make sure we are safe and that we are moving forward toward a better future. I know I've probably got two of the best parents ever.

If I ever forget that, all I have to do is remember the time when Mom came with me to the state championship in Saratoga Springs.

We started out at the car rental place that's not far from the school. When we got there, we saw my best friend, Zixi, with Coach Russ and Coach Shawn and Coach Angel and Coach Nashali and Coach Aaron and Coach Logan. Then the whole team and all the coaches and my mom and I climbed into a white van and drove for hours and hours and hours.

On the way it got dark outside pretty quickly, and everyone was either talking or listening to music. Mom was sitting in the back, laughing with some of the coaches, and I liked the way that it seemed like she was on the team, just like me.

I was sitting right behind Coach Shawn, and he pulled out his phone and started playing a game online. I watched and saw that it was a live game. I tried not to talk and to just let him play, but after two moves I was so full of questions that I thought I might burst.

I said, "Coach Shawn, who are you playing?"

He said it was a live game organized by some people in Chicago. And because Coach Shawn says that he likes for me to ask questions, and he has never told me to stop, I asked him a whole bunch more.

"Why did you make that first move? Is that a new opening? What's it called? What rating is the person you're playing? Do you think they're a master like you? Did you ever play Fabiano? What happened?"

Coach Shawn answered all of my questions, and he only once said, "Don't you want to take a nap, kid?"

I was super excited and so I said, "No, Coach Shawn! I'm not at all tired." And I kept on asking him questions.

When we finally stopped driving, I was starting to almost feel tired, but Coach Russ showed Mom and me into the house he had rented and said that we were going to have the biggest room because Mom was the guest of honor. It was a *really* big room, and I think you could have put four of the rooms from The Hotel into that one.

Mom said it was late and that I should go to sleep, but I was excited again, so I went downstairs because the coaches were all sitting around playing chess and laughing. I asked Coach Shawn if I could stay up and play, but he gave me a look like the one Mom had given him outside the airport and said, "You want to do well in this tournament?"

I nodded and said, "Yes, Coach Shawn."

"Then you better get your butt to sleep."

I didn't argue at all. I went straight to bed.

42 | THE FIRST MATCH

OLUWATOYIN ————

On the first day of the state championship the room felt just like it always did in every other tournament I had been to. Parents and coaches talked, our children came and went, and the atmosphere was calm.

I always like these moments. I like to watch the way the coaches help the players to find their focus and prepare them to go out and play their best. I like the way they tell stories and give their players advice so that they will do well in life as well as chess.

Coach Shawn started that morning with a question.

"Imagine I take you out of this room and magically drop you off in France. You don't have a cell phone, you don't have a map, and you can't speak the language. What's the one word that best describes how you feel?"

Tani and the others put their hands up and said the same thing. "Lost!"

"That's right," said Coach Shawn. "And it's exactly the same with chess. You might have spent hours and hours studying your openings and remembering the moves you want to make, but if you decide to deviate from your plan and start moving pieces without thinking just because you want to hurry things along and get the game finished, it's like landing in another country. You'll feel lost, and it will all be because you stopped thinking and started rushing."

Soon after that, it was time for the first round of matches. Tani came over to say goodbye and have a hug, but I could tell that his mind was already in the match room.

"Are you okay?" I asked.

He mumbled something about not wanting to end up in France, then turned and strode toward the door.

Tani plays fast. Sometimes too fast. He says that he likes to make his moves quickly and aggressively like Paul Morphy did, but Coach Russ is always trying to have him slow down. Coach Russ says that if he's moving so fast that he's knocking pieces over or isn't putting them down in the middle of the square, he's got to slow down.

All the same, tournament matches can take as long as two or three hours, even in third grade. So when Tani left for his first match, I settled back and prepared to wait.

My mind drifted.

Minutes slipped into each other.

And then Tani was standing in the doorway.

His face was blank, like it always is when he finishes a match. The only way of telling how he's done is to watch his right hand.

Slowly he lifted his arm and stuck out his fist. Then he stuck out his thumb and jabbed it into the air.

"Well done!" said Coach Russ.

"High five!" said Coach Shawn.

And me? I got another hug.

43 | THREE BIG THUMBS-UP

TANI ————————

Even though the tournament was bigger than anything I'd ever been to in New York and there was a lot of noise and distractions like there were in Orlando, I stuck to my plan all through my first game. I took it slow. Really slow. I remembered my opening and saw the board take on the patterns that I wanted it to. I stayed calm and breathed steadily, and after a long time of playing, I won.

It was the same with the second game. I went in knowing that the number one main thing I did not want to do was to rush. Or lose.

I *won*.

"Okay, my man," said Coach Shawn as he finished looking through my notebook after the second match. "This is good, but let's not make a big deal of this. Keep working on those openings."

That's what I did. I used a laptop and practiced my favorite openings. I'd done it before a lot of times, but it felt good to remind myself of how the board should look if I was making the best possible choices.

Soon I was playing my third game.

That one was quick.

When I came back into the team room after my third game and held my thumb up high so that Coach Shawn and Mom could both see that I'd won, it felt extra good.

Mom gave me a hug, and Coach Shawn held up his hand for a high five. "Nice work, Tani. You're 3–0. If this were a one-day tournament, you'd have won."

We went back to the house soon after and had some food. I really, really wanted to stay up and play with the coaches, especially as they were playing blitz and the room was full of laughter and the coaches were saying funny things to each other. I begged Coach Shawn, and he actually said yes. "But just one game of blitz, and then you gotta go to bed straight after. Agreed?"

We played and he won. He's really good, and so he got me with this trap that I didn't see until the last minute. It was the first match I'd lost all day, but I didn't mind.

Before I said good night, he said, "Tani, you have a shot at actually winning this tournament now. So get some sleep and be ready for a big day, okay?"

I said, "Yes, Coach Shawn," and ran up the stairs to bed. It had been a great day, but I really liked the idea of the next day being even better.

44 | WONDERING AND WAITING

OLUWATOYIN ────────

Tani wasn't the only one who started the second day of the state championship with the maximum points. A boy from a different school who also studied under Coach Russ was 3–0, and there were several more who had only dropped half a point by drawing one and winning two.

As soon as I walked into the room early on Sunday morning, it felt different. Across the room little huddles of children gathered around their coaches. There were tables full of snacks and drinks, but nobody had time for that. There was work to be done.

I liked watching Coach Shawn run through his pregame routine with his players from P.S. 116. This time there were no knight pieces handed out, but there was a lot of talk about lions.

"That's what you all are," he said. "You're my lions, and I'm proud of you. Now come on in here and let's get one of you in the middle so that we can send you out onto the wide-open savanna to go hunting. Who's first?"

The room filled with the sound of chanting as first Tani and then the other players from P.S. 116 were placed in the middle.

Saturday's matches had all been long by Tani's standards, some of them over two hours. So soon after he went off to play his first match of the day, I settled into a chair and sat quietly reading my book. I'd only made it through a few pages when Coach Russ came and joined me. I couldn't hold in my question for very long.

"Coach Russ, how do you think Tani will do today?"

He leaned forward and rubbed his hands together. "You've got to understand how tough this tournament is. New York represents the best scholastic chess players in the country. Tani's going up against the best and brightest."

Then he shrugged.

"But there's something about Tani that's special. It's not because of where he's come from—I've seen other kids come from similar backgrounds and other kids who have learned how to play quickly. What's unique about Tani is Tani. People are drawn to him, and everybody who meets him loves him. He's put himself at the table with players who are way better than him, players at the national level, and he just seems to fit right in. So, will he do well today? I think so. He nearly lost his last match yesterday, so he's still got to battle to keep his focus right, but could he end up in the top four or five? I think he could."

"Can he win the whole thing?"

"Yes," he smiled. "It would be a miracle though."

Tani came back from his fourth match with his thumb raised high and his smile as bright as ever. He went through his notation book with Coach Shawn, and in between doing puzzles and talking with the coaches, I made sure he had something to eat and drink.

The room felt different when he went out for his fifth game. Some of the other parents had left already, after their children had been eliminated, and so the place was quieter. I tried reading my book, but I had no appetite for it. All I wanted to do was sit quietly and enjoy the calm as each minute ticked by.

I sniffed and felt something on my nose. It was blood. Quite a lot of it too. I went to the bathroom, used some tissue to get the bleeding under control, and cleaned myself up.

While I was washing, the most powerful memory hit me. The last time I'd had a nosebleed was the day I gave birth to Tani. It had taken a long time to stop it then, but the midwife had told me it was normal and that I should not worry about it.

I stayed in the bathroom, the memory so real that I could almost feel the tightening in my belly again. I remembered the way the bed felt, the bright hospital lights, the sound of other babies and women crying out nearby.

And then I remembered the song that I'd been singing the day Tani came into the world. It was a song that we sang at church about God taking a little shepherd boy named David and making him a great and mighty king.

I sang it quietly to myself again as I walked back to the team room.

45 | DOING DEEP THINKING

TANI ————

If you want to be good at chess, there are some things that you have to be able to do. You have to be able to concentrate on the board for a long time. You have to remember all the moves for your opening. You have to know how you're going to respond to different traps that your opponent is going to try and lay for you. All these things are all really important. But they're not enough. There's one thing that you cannot survive without if you want to win: you have to be able to do deep thinking.

Coach Shawn is always telling us, "You can't just find a move. You have to *have plans*." He says, "This is what chess comes down to. Can you gather all the possible detail of a position and then come up with a move that is either going to fix your weakness or increase your strength?"

Every Thursday he talks about this. And when he does, he always sets us a challenge. He puts a position up on the whiteboard and says, "Okay, guys, imagine you find yourself right here in a game. I'm putting fifteen minutes on the clock, and you've got to find me three plans for how to get out of here."

Those fifteen minutes are tough. We have to think ahead four or five moves, and while we're trying to do that, Coach Shawn walks around reminding us what to do, saying things like, "Look for those candidate choices, people!" or "How's the king looking?" or "What's the pawn structure? What's your weakness? What needs to improve?"

The time always goes by really fast. And when it does, Coach Shawn asks each of us to say what we think. We have to tell him which of our plans is the best and why. Sometimes he even asks us what plan we'd use if our opponent was really aggressive or really defensive.

It's hard work.

But it's how you learn to do deep thinking.

In my fifth game at the state championship I was staring at the board, and I could almost hear Coach Shawn ask me to tell him about the pawns and the king and the weaknesses in my position and everything else. I was looking ahead maybe six or even seven moves, and I'd never done that before in a game. I was trying to hold on to the thought and not let my brain get distracted at all by anything other than the position and the moves ahead.

And then I remembered playing a Paul Morphy game, and I knew that if I could get my opponent to take my bishop, I could win.

46 | MOVES LIKE A LION

OLUWATOYIN ───────────

I heard Tani before I could see him or spot which way his thumb was pointing. He was laughing as he burst through the door, walking side by side with his opponent.

"I know!" he said. "You thought I'd blundered when you took my bishop and I just took your pawn, didn't you?"

His opponent laughed a little, too, then went to join his parents. It was only then that Tani stuck his thumb up at Coach Shawn and me.

I pulled him close and gave him a hug. "Did you say a thank-you to God?"

"Thank You, God! Thank You, God! Thank You, God!"

"Well done. Now, I think Coach Shawn wants to talk to you."

Tani rushed over to the coaches, high-fiving and fist-bumping them all.

I sat back and listened. I was expecting there to be a lot of talk about him being 5–0, and perhaps some words about there only being one more game, but they were quiet. Quieter than usual. Coach Shawn and some of the others were looking at Tani's notation book.

"Why did you do that?" said Coach Shawn. "Sacrificing your bishop for a pawn like that. It's not what I would have expected."

"And there's another way," said Coach Russ. "A simpler one that could have got you to the same place in the end. Did you see it?"

Tani smiled. "I wanted to sacrifice the bishop. I'd seen it before and wanted to try it."

"Where?" said Coach Shawn.

"It was one of Paul Morphy's games. I can't remember which one though."

The conversation moved on, and Tani went to the bathroom. When he came back, Coach Shawn was pointing at his laptop. He had added all of the moves into the program and got it to the point where Tani was about to make the controversial move.

"You were right," he said, pointing to the screen. "I put the game in, and the computer agrees that the strongest move you could make at this point is to sacrifice your bishop. That earned you eighty points right there."

Tani looked surprised. "Eighty points? Wow!"

Coach Shawn nodded. "You're my lion, all right. It's aggressive and unorthodox. It's pure Paul Morphy."

47 | THE LAST GAME

TANI ————

I was so pleased that I was 5–0. I wasn't even thinking about the state championship. I was just really, really pleased that I'd been able to think deeper than I'd ever thought before.

The coaches talked about me sacrificing the bishop for some time, but when they were finished, they said it was really good. I think Coach Shawn was most pleased of all because he held up his hand again to give me five. He had the biggest smile possible on his face as he said, "This is gonna hurt!" And when he gave me five it *really did hurt*, but I was still laughing and so happy about everything that I didn't mind.

Pretty soon I started to think about the next game. The last game. The only game I needed to win in order to win the tournament. For the first time that weekend I could feel the nerves going a bit crazy inside of me.

Coach Shawn had told me to study, and so I found a small space in the corner near where he was sitting and looked at the chess program on his laptop. It lets you put in your moves and then tells you which is the very best move you can make from that position.

"That's good," said Coach Shawn. "Keep on putting your game in and memorize what the app is telling you. If you're sticking to the number one choice, that will be enough."

It was hard to really concentrate because the room around me was so loud. But it was loud inside me too. I was feeling nervous.

I was also feeling confused because someone had said to me, "You don't need to win. You just need to draw." I had five points because I'd won every game, but my opponent had won four and drawn one, so he had four and a half points. If we drew, I'd have five and a half and he'd have five. I understood that all I needed was half a point to beat him, but I'd never really played to draw before. I'd always played to win.

The hall was quiet when I went in to play the last game. Normally there were lots of games being played at the same time, but because it was right at the end of the tournament, there were only two other games being played. I liked the quiet because it helped me think.

I still had to work hard to concentrate on my game. The biggest distraction was the fact that I was playing someone I knew already. Jack Oliver Faissal goes to a different school and doesn't come to any of the chess programs I go to, but I met him at summer camp, and I like him.

I was the black chess pieces, and I started the way I wanted to. I'd done exactly what Coach Shawn said and memorized the moves I wanted to make as well as the best moves that white should make. Sometimes Jack made the best move, but a lot of the time he didn't. I had the center of the board controlled, and I knew that I was going to win. Maybe it would take five more moves or maybe ten. But I knew it. And when I saw him look at the board and hold in his breath and move his hand a few times but not touch a piece, I knew that he was feeling worried. He was nervous, and he knew that I was in a strong position. Coach Shawn talks a lot about playing the player and not just the pieces. Seeing him get nervous and unsure of himself like that made me feel really good.

On my fourteenth move I did something really simple that was going to help me really break into his pawns. I moved my queen to G6.

I let go of the queen and sat back to think some more about what he might do and how I could respond.

Immediately I realized something that made me feel sick.

Moving the queen like that had been a blunder. Not a little blunder or a small mistake. It was a really, really big blunder. The biggest one I'd ever made. I'd opened a door that would ruin everything. If my opponent looked hard enough and saw it, then he'd probably be able to beat me in fewer than four moves.

I could feel my mouth get completely dry. The more I stared at the board, the more I could see that I was lost. Totally lost. There was no way that I could play my way out. It was over.

Unless I could get a draw.

I made myself sit up straight and smile, and I stuck my hand out and said in my most confident voice, "I offer a draw."

He looked at me hard. He was trying to read me. I kept my eyes on his and waved my hand to remind him that I wanted him to shake it. I didn't want him to look at the board, because if he did, he might see that he could win.

He opened his mouth to speak, then said, "I accept."

We shook hands, and I walked back to the team room. I felt bad. I didn't like that I'd drawn, and I really didn't like that I'd made such a blunder.

Everyone was staring at me as I came in. I held a fist up and stuck my thumb out sideways. I felt heavy and slow and not at all happy. Coach Shawn came over to me and held out his hands. I said, "I drew."

He grabbed me. He asked, "Do you know what you just did?"

I said, "Yes, I drew. It was a tough game."

"But you drew! That means you won! You're the New York State champion!"

Then he shouted out so loud that I thought my ears might burst, "Tani drew! He's the champion!"

Coach Russ shouted to me, "Tani!" and picked me up and held me so high in the air that I thought I was going to hit the roof. "You're state champion. You won!"

I said, "I did? But I really blundered, and he was going to beat me."

"But he didn't," Coach Russ said.

Just then the door opened again, and my friend Zixi came in. He was smiling, and his coach ran over to him, and he started shouting to the room that he'd won his age group division too.

I could feel the excitement start to burst inside me like fireworks. All the nerves and all the bad feelings about not winning suddenly disappeared. Instead, I felt so great and excited and happy that I joined Zixi in doing a really long floss dance that was so good all the coaches and adults in the room were laughing so hard they were nearly crying.

Mom came over, and when she'd finished giving me a hug, she looked at me. She didn't have to remind me because I was already chanting, "Thank You, God! Thank You, God! Thank You, God!"

48 | A TROPHY AS TALL AS TANI

KAYODE ————————

"Wow!"

That was all I could say as I held my phone and stared at the screen. So I said it again. "Wow!"

I was watching the video that Oluwatoyin was sending me, live. Austin was crowded in next to me, and I could feel that he was just as excited as I was.

On the small screen Tani was holding out his hands to receive a trophy that was almost as tall as he was. His smile was as wide as I'd ever seen it, and the noise of cheering and shouting was cracking through the speaker.

"You won! You're state champion," I said when the cheering had died down a little and we were able to talk to him ourselves. I was hardly able to believe it.

Austin smiled at him. "I knew you'd do it," he said. "I'm proud of you, little brother."

Before we could talk much more the call cut out.

But our smiles lasted for hours.

49 | A STORY WORTH SHARING

OLUWATOYIN ——————

Tani was exhausted. For the first hour of the journey back from Saratoga Springs to the city he tried to resist sleep, but the tiredness finally won, and he soon lay slumped against me. It was midnight by the time we pulled up on Park Avenue outside the shelter, and I wondered whether I was going to have to carry him into the elevator. But once the van filled with cold air he woke, saw his giant trophy, and sprang back to life.

The next day was a regular Monday. There were all the usual chores to do, the usual bags to pack, and there was the usual homework to remember. Kayode left early to catch the city's first commuters as they arrived at nearby Grand Central, and Austin had an early basketball practice. Miss Maria handed Tani a doughnut before I took him to school, and we talked about the day ahead as we walked. It was only as we reached the school gate that Tani mentioned anything having to do with chess.

"Do you think they'll let me bring my trophy to school, Mom?"

I told him that I was sure they would, and we said goodbye.

I was nearly back to the shelter when Coach Russ called. His voice was hoarse, and he sounded like he had been talking all night, but he was still full of excitement.

"Mrs. Adewumi, are you still living in the homeless shelter on Park Avenue?"

"Yes, Coach Russ."

"Okay. Well, I was thinking that maybe I could talk to some people about you and see if I can get a journalist to share your story. Would you be willing to talk to someone about Tani's progress in chess and how you had to leave Nigeria?"

"Do you think anyone would be interested? Do people even want to read about chess players?"

"You'd be surprised. A few years ago, I coached another kid whose family were hardworking immigrants from Bangladesh. The boy had played a little chess before but not a whole lot. Within two years he was the best player in the country in his age group. The kid got offered a place in one of the best private schools in the country, and he went on to win four national championships."

I was impressed. "But winning the nationals and winning the state tournament are not the same, are they?"

"That's true, but there's something about your story that I think people will connect with. Maybe talk it over with your husband and let me know what you think."

I did just that. Kayode was like me at first, unsure that anyone would be interested enough to write about Tani. It wasn't that we were not proud of what he'd done—we were—but we knew that there were other children who had higher scores and more trophies than Tani. And as for being a hard-working refugee family, well, we knew that New York was full of people just like us. The way we saw it, there was nothing too unusual about the story.

"But," I said to Kayode, "I think Coach Russ is right when he says that the press likes stories about chess players." As well as the family from Bangladesh, Coach Russ had told me about another chess player whose story went public. I had spent some time googling him and was so inspired.

The man was named Majur Juac, and he was from Sudan in East Africa. When he was seven, the war that had been raging in his country for years finally reached his village. Rebel soldiers sent him and many of the other boys in the village away, and they walked for two days without stopping, not knowing where they were going. Their journey continued, and they walked for months, covering hundreds of miles until they arrived in Ethiopia. But when the government there was overthrown, they were forced to turn around and walk all the way back to Sudan.

For a total of five years he walked. It was a dangerous journey, and he saw so much death that it lost the power to shock him. When he finally settled in a refugee camp in Kenya, he had to struggle to survive on a handful of food each day.

When he was nineteen years old, some aid workers gave the refugees a chess set. Majur would watch the Sudanese soldiers play during the day, studying the game. Then at night, when the men were out, he and a friend would quietly enter the game room, set up the board, and play.

In time he was invited to live in America and was granted asylum. He took a job as a security guard in a grocery store but played chess in his spare time. Eventually he ended in up New York, working for Coach Russ. Several newspapers told his story, and as I read the comments that readers left at the bottom of each article, I understood a little more why Coach Russ thought that a journalist might want to tell Tani's story.

Majur's journey shone bright in my mind. But it wasn't the only one. In my searching I discovered another article about a gifted chess player in New York whose life was transformed by the game. But this time, the player was not a stranger to me. It was Coach Shawn. And yet the sixteen-year-old Shawn Martinez described in the *New York Times* piece from 2007 was almost completely different from the Coach Shawn whom Tani adored.

The article called him a teenage riddle. Shawn skipped months of school, and on the day he was supposed to represent his school as they tried to retain their national high school title, he was nowhere near the tournament. Instead, he was on Wall Street, playing blitz chess with the bankers for ten dollars a game.

The article told of Shawn's early life, how he had been removed from his mother when he was one week old and adopted by a woman named Lidia Martinez. His father had died when Shawn was two, and much of his life, the article said, had been difficult.

But the thing that surprised me more than anything else was the fact that Shawn told the interviewer that he had never read a chess book. He said they were boring.

I could not imagine Coach Shawn ever talking like that. I had been in more than enough team rooms and midweek sessions to know that Coach Shawn always encouraged his students to push themselves hard. He was always urging them to work hard, to study, to learn from the masters of the past. I could recognize the beginnings of Coach Shawn in the description of Shawn Martinez, just like I could recognize him in the photo. But whatever happened in the twelve years between the article and the present day must have been dramatic.

Reading these two articles changed my opinion about Tani being interviewed by a journalist. Perhaps if Coach Russ could persuade someone to run a story, no matter how small the number of readers, maybe just one of them might be inspired and encouraged by Tani's story.

Once I'd told him about what I'd read, Kayode agreed, and I phoned Coach Russ back to tell him to please go ahead and begin his search for a journalist.

"That's great news," he said. "And I've been wondering about something else too. If we can get the story out there, would you like me to set up a fundraising page for you?"

He was on speakerphone. Kayode and I looked at each other, confused.

"Fundraising for what, Coach Russ?" said Kayode.

"To help you guys move out of the shelter. Maybe we can raise $10,000 and help you move on somewhere. What do you think?"

I thought it was ridiculous. Nobody was going to give us $10,000, no matter how good the article was. The whole thing was a waste of time.

Kayode had a different concern. "We have never begged. All this time that we have been in America, we have never begged. I do not wish to start now."

"That's okay," said Coach Russ. "It won't be like that. I promise. I can be the one doing the asking instead of you. Would that be okay?"

We were quiet. Kayode looked thoughtful, then surprised me by saying that he was happy with that.

"And you, Mrs. Adewumi? Are you okay with it?"

"If my husband is happy, and you think it is worthwhile, I am."

"That's great," said Coach Russ. "And if none of this works out, then we'll hold a fundraiser in the school and see if we can raise enough money to get you out of the shelter and into a studio apartment."

We didn't hear again from Coach Russ for the rest of that Monday. He did send us some messages saying he was still working on it but that he had not yet been able to find anyone to take the story.

It wasn't until Tuesday afternoon that he phoned.

"Are you ready for that interview?"

I said I was, though my guess was that after trying for more than one whole day, whoever he had been able to persuade to do the interview would not be writing for a popular newspaper.

"Great. He wants to interview you all at P.S. 116 on Thursday morning. He's named Nicholas Kristof, and he writes for the *New York Times*. You should google him first."

I thanked him and did what he said.

"Wow," I said quietly when I saw that he had won not one but two Pulitzer Prizes. "He's impressive."

50 | AN OUTPOURING OF GENEROSITY

KAYODE ———————

I parked the car, turned off the engine, and stared at the web page on my phone.

"This 8-Year-Old Chess Champion Will Make You Smile."

The second I saw the photo of Tani staring at a chessboard on the *New York Times* website, I had tears in my eyes. There was a smile on my face as well, especially as I read on.

Nicholas Kristof had written a perfect summary of Tani's story. He explained our situation correctly and had great quotes from so many of the people who had helped Tani along the way. Tani's school principal called it "an inspiring example of how life's challenges do not define a person." Coach Russ said, "Tani is rich beyond measure." Mr. Kristof even ended with my own words: "The U.S. is a dream country. . . . Thank God I live in the greatest city in the world, which is New York, New York."

What I liked most about the piece was the single-line summary right at the top. "Overcoming life's basic truth: Talent is universal, but opportunity is not."[1]

"Yes!" I said to my empty car. "That is the truth!" Ever since the Boko Haram militants visited my printshop and tracked me down to my home, we had experienced the slow suffocation of opportunity. The opportunity to work, to earn, to live freely, and to dream. All of those had been taken from us in Nigeria.

It was the same story in Dallas too. The opportunity to belong to the family, to find work and make a new life for ourselves—that was held back as well.

Without opportunity, life had grown weak. It had become a shadow of what it was, a pale imitation of what it could be.

New York had changed all that. A homeless shelter was all the opportunity we needed to build a home. A six-dollar-an-hour job washing pans was all the opportunity I needed to build my work again. And the community of chess coaches and church friends was all we needed to build a new family again.

The article was a triumph. Even though we had only spent an hour or so with him the day before, I felt as though Nicholas Kristof knew us and understood our story with the greatest wisdom and insight possible.

I read the piece through again.

And again.

When I reached the end for the third time, I noticed something I had not seen before. It wasn't just Oluwatoyin, me, and Coach Russ who had read the piece. Someone else who I had never heard of before had left a comment. It said, "An inspiring, well-timed, true story to remind Americans of who we aspire to be."[2]

"Moving and uplifting," wrote another reader. "The side of our nation we all need to celebrate and promote."[3]

"All too often, our society discourages aspiration, especially for kids with darker skins. We are blessed to have Tani and others like him who don't want to give up."[4]

They kept on coming. More and more comments, and all of them positive, all of them saying the same thing—that Tani's story had touched them.

Coach Russ phoned me. He was laughing so hard that I struggled to understand him at first. "It's crazy, isn't it?" he said. "But just wait. I've set up the GoFundMe page, and Nick Kristof says he's going to put a link to it at the bottom of the piece. Let's see what happens then."

I was at home by the time the link appeared on the *New York Times* piece. It took readers through to the page that Coach Russ had set up. It explained a little of Tani's story, including that we were living in a homeless shelter. "Tani IS ALL HEART!" wrote Coach Russ. "Let's all show our HEART and help Tani's family secure a home where he can continue on his journey."[5]

Coach Russ had put the target at $25,000. Oluwatoyin and I had both agreed that this was a lot of money and that even if we achieved just half that amount, we would be so, so happy. But just as with the comments on the article, people started to donate to the appeal.

Within thirty minutes we had raised more than $1,000.

In an hour we were above $3,000.

And by the time four hours had passed and I was ready for bed, the $10,000 target had already been met. I looked closely. Some of the donations were large, as much as $100 or more, but almost all of them were $5, $10, or $15.

Throughout the next day, whenever I was not driving, I checked the *New York Times* piece and the GoFundMe page. The comments and contributions were both rising steadily, and every time I checked, the numbers left me amazed and awestruck.

Coach Russ called in the afternoon. "I think we've got to increase the target. What do you think about $50,000?"

I was still stunned by the whole thing. "That is a lot of money," I replied, "but if you think it's the right thing to do, then I trust you."

"I really do. This is connecting with people in such a deep way. And I don't think it's anywhere near being done yet."

He was right. Increasing the target did not stop the donations. If anything, they seemed to be coming in even faster. And it wasn't just the GoFundMe page or the article that was attracting attention. I started to receive Facebook messages from journalists and producers who wanted to talk to us. Coach Russ had them, too, and soon we had a list of people to call back from NY1, CNN, and NBC. Even President Clinton's office made contact and asked if we could schedule a time to visit him.

One week after the piece was first posted online, the story was still going. If anything, it was bigger than ever. The smaller donations were still coming in, but most days there were also some big ones as well, donations so big that I struggled to believe it. Several people and groups donated $1,000, two people donated $5,000, and two even gave $10,000.

The story went international. We had calls from TV stations in Germany and Japan, Mexico and China. The BBC in London wanted to meet, the Canadian government sent a beautiful chessboard, and a friend back home in Nigeria told me that most newspapers and TV stations carried the story, which then led to Tani's name being discussed in the senate in Nigeria, where the president was urged to acknowledge his success and give him honor. I even heard that in Morocco they passed a law that all schoolchildren should be taught chess.

We said yes to more than fifteen of these interview requests, and soon we were almost familiar with the questions we were asked.

But then, two weeks in, I received a call from Coach Russ that left me shocked and speechless.

"I've taken two calls this morning," he said. "And you're not going to believe what's happened. Are you driving? You should pull over."

He paused while I told him I needed to find somewhere to park. I could hear the blood rushing in my ears. I forced myself to concentrate on taking the car safely to the side of the road.

"I am parked now. What is it? Is it bad news?"

"No, it's not bad news. It's the most amazing news we've heard yet. Someone e-mailed me this morning, and they're offering to buy you a car. Brand new."

He let the words hang for a moment.

"But that's not all. I've just had a call from someone else. He wants to pay your rent for a year. Kayode, you're getting out of the shelter. You hear me?"

I heard him. I heard him loud and clear. But at that moment I could say nothing in reply. All I could do was shake my head and offer a prayer of thanks.

51 | A TV STUDIO SURPRISE

TANI ———————

Being interviewed on TV is confusing.

I had never been in a TV studio before, so there was a lot to look at. In part of the room the lights were up really bright, but in other parts it was really dark. People were busy running around and talking, and I was told to sit on a couch with Coach Russ and Coach Shawn. Because I don't watch TV, I didn't know who the other people sitting opposite me were. But they seemed nice.

Someone told everyone to be quiet, and it was like magic. The room went silent, and the people on the other sofa froze and stared at one of the TV cameras.

A lady said something about how I was "eight years old and well on the way to mastering the extremely difficult game of chess." I wasn't sure about that. I was at 1,562 right then, but before I could call myself a master, I'd need to increase my score to something like 2,200 or more. I didn't say anything, though, because she stopped talking and everything went quiet while the picture of me with the trophy from the state championship came on lots of the TV screens in the studio. Then we all watched a video about me. They'd filmed it at the Thursday chess club, and it said I was a "chess champion capturing hearts," but I wasn't sure about that either. All I knew was that I hadn't played very well when the cameras were pointed at me, and I wondered if maybe someone would spot that.

The video kept on playing, and I tried to remember the questions that the people in the studio had said they were going to ask me.

By this time, I'd already been interviewed by lots of different people. Like Mr. Nicholas, who came to see me at school right after the state championship. He was the first one I spoke to, and he wrote about what had happened to me and my family and how Coach Russ and Coach Shawn had helped me learn how to play properly. He wanted to know what life was like living in the shelter, and I liked him and was glad that lots of people were reading what he wrote.

There had been other interviews with other people as well. Sometimes people asked me about life in Nigeria, but I could never really answer those questions because of not remembering much about it. I liked it most when people asked me about chess. Whenever anyone asked me what I liked about the game I'd say, "It teaches you how to think. When you play, something happens in your brain, and you see all these lines that you could take, and you have to look for the best one." And if I was asked, "How do you feel when you lose?" I would say, "When you lose you lose, and when you win you win. It's a game. That's all."

When the video ended, the TV studio was quiet again, and everyone was looking at me. The lights seemed super bright, and I wanted to look around, but something told me that I needed to concentrate really hard and look at the woman who was talking to me. She said, "How did you feel when you won that championship?"

I said, "I felt surprised."

She said, "Did you? You couldn't believe you got that good that fast?"

I didn't know what to say to that. She had answered my question for me, but she got the answer wrong. The correct answer was that when I won the championship, I felt surprised because I drew, and a draw didn't feel like a win, but the interviewer was now asking questions to Coach Russ and Coach Shawn, so I guessed they didn't need me to keep talking.

I was looking around me. There was this big green wall behind us, and on the TV screens I could see that pictures of me and my family were showing. That was weird.

But then I heard Coach Shawn talking about the game in Saratoga Springs where I sacrificed the bishop. He said that was a master-level idea. That made me feel really good inside.

They had a chessboard on the table in front of me, and they asked me to show them how I would start a game. I got checkmate in three moves, but I don't think they were concentrating really hard.

So with the questions and the game and the green wall behind me, it was all kind of confusing. But it was good too. Especially when Coach Russ announced that, as soon as we finished up in the TV studio, my family and I were going to move into our new apartment.

He said, "Tani is no longer homeless!"

Everybody clapped, and I felt so happy that I didn't know where to look.

52 | OPPORTUNITY FOR OTHERS

KAYODE

In this life it is not easy to get money. Even if you do not have terrorists visiting your office in the day or trying to break down the door to your house at night, it is difficult to make your way forward. Even if you have your own home with your own door key and your own family around to support and encourage and nurture you, making money is tough.

If you want to succeed you cannot be lazy. Hard work is essential. You must be prepared to sweat, to serve, to put aside your ego and forget about the notion that you are somehow above a certain type of job. If you want to make it, you must be prepared to persevere where others will give up.

But being able to push yourself to keep going is not always enough. If you are going to thrive, you will need someone to see your potential and invest in you. Because, as Mr. Nicholas Kristof wrote, talent is universal; opportunity is not.

Oluwatoyin and I stood beside Austin in the NBC studios while Tani, Coach Russ, and Coach Shawn were interviewed live on the *Today* show. We had spent the whole week doing interviews, but this was special. It was an unforgettable joy to see Tani celebrated like this and hear Coach Russ announce to the world that once we left the studio, we were going to move into the apartment that an anonymous donor had agreed to fund for a whole year.

The GoFundMe page was already well over $100,000. With millions of people watching the show, we knew that this figure was sure to increase. It was obvious that this was a clear and great opportunity.

Our motivation for agreeing to the GoFundMe page had always been simple: we wanted to be able to move out of the homeless shelter and into a home of our own. Thanks to the generosity of one man, we no longer had that need. The other person who offered to buy a brand-new car was making the final arrangements regarding insurance, and we had even been approached by lawyers offering to work for us pro bono as we sought our green cards.

So many of our needs had been met, and we saw that this was now an opportunity that went beyond just our family.

As we left the studio and headed south toward our new home on the Lower East Side, I decided to tell Coach Russ about something that Oluwatoyin and I had been talking about. "We want to give back," I said. "There are so many people out there who need help."

"Not everyone can set up a GoFundMe page or talk to the press or go on TV," said Oluwatoyin. "And not everyone has a church to help them or can get to PATH or has kind chess coaches who pay for their son's fees or schools that give winter coats. We want to do something for those people."

Coach Russ was quiet as we walked. I wondered whether he would be upset.

"We're not ungrateful," I said. "We appreciate all the kindness that people have shown in giving so much money. And we are so grateful to you for setting it up in the first place. But this money can help so many people. Do you understand what I am saying?"

"I do." He nodded but fell silent again. "I really do."

53 | A PLACE OF OUR OWN

TANI ——————

When we got to the apartment, we started shouting. Not bad shouting but good shouting. Really good shouting. The kind of shouting you do when you're so happy, it's as if all the fireworks in the world are exploding inside you.

Dad started it as soon as he opened the door. He said, "Wow! Wow! Wow!"

Then Mom joined in, saying, "This is too much!"

Austin and I ran from the kitchen to the living room to the hallway to the first bedroom, then we ran from the second bedroom to the bathroom. We both had the biggest grins on our faces you've ever seen and were shouting things like "This is amazing!" and "I can't believe it!"

When Austin and I came back into the living room, Mom and Dad and Coach Russ were on their knees in the empty room. They were crying and praying at the same time.

Dad was saying, "God, You are too much. Wow! I know that You fed the five thousand and You parted the Red Sea, but this? It's too marvelous. Thank You!"

Mom prayed too. "It doesn't matter if this place stays empty forever! Thank You, God!"

Austin and I were kneeling down too. All I could say was, "Thank You, God! Thank You, God! Thank You, God!" The more I said it, the more excited I felt. This was *our home*!

Now I need to tell you that our living room is a big room, especially when there's no furniture. For over a year we had been living in the two bedrooms in The Hotel, and they were really small. The living room was about a hundred times bigger, so I stopped kneeling and started rolling around on the floor. I couldn't control myself. I was just so excited.

Then Mom and Dad and Austin and I think even Coach Russ joined in. Rolling around on the floor, laughing and saying, "Thank You!"

Later, after we had stopped rolling and laughing so hard, Mr. Nicholas came by with a photographer. He was so excited for us and had a smile on his face easily as big as mine or Austin's. The photographer asked if he could take a picture of me and I said yes. He asked if there was anywhere in particular I wanted to be, and I knew right away. I wanted to be in the bedroom, lying on my new bed.

There's one thing that I never got to tell anyone in an interview about what it's like to play chess. I never told them how my head feels when I've finished a tournament. After all that deep thinking my head hurts. Often all I want to do is get home and go to sleep.

So when I lay on the big, comfortable bed in the big, comfortable bedroom and let the photographer take his pictures, I was thinking one thing. I was imagining how great it would be to come home from a tournament even with a sore head and lie down and sleep on this bed.

54 | PAYING IT FORWARD

OLUWATOYIN ————————

"Our Chess Champion Has a Home."[6]

That was the headline of the article that Nicholas Kristof wrote the following weekend. It featured a picture of Tani lying on the bed, staring out of the window. And while the first article went viral and was one of the most shared stories of the whole year on the *New York Times* website, this second piece did not. Instead it brought the story to an end.

It was right that it did.

We had just lived through the strangest period of our lives. For ten straight days Tani's story was all the media seemed to want. It was one of the most shared stories in the world. The coverage was uninterrupted, and politicians from all over the world discussed Tani's story. We had approaches from book publishers and agents and film producers. Lawyers approached us and offered their services without charge. We even spent over an hour talking happily with former president Bill Clinton in his office. Tani did most of the talking, naturally.

By then it was time for life to return to something like normal.

There were just two things we knew that we had to do.

First, with the total raised now over $250,000, we knew that it was time to post an update on the GoFundMe site and share our plan with everyone who had been so kind and given to the campaign. We explained that what had started as a need for a home had become something far bigger. The outpouring of generosity from people all over the world had been far greater than we could have ever imagined. We shared that our housing and other needs had been met by people outside of GoFundMe and explained that because of this we felt compelled to do something equally great with the money that had been given. We wanted to give other people the same opportunity we had received, to see their lives transformed. So we wrote that the campaign would accept donations for a further twenty-four hours and then begin transferring funds to the Tanitoluwa Adewumi Foundation.

We both wondered whether people would be unhappy about our change. We explained that we understood that people did not necessarily donate to our campaign with this new purpose in mind. We had discussed it with GoFundMe and posted a link if people wanted their money returned.

With the help of lawyers and others, we began the process of registering the Tanitoluwa Adewumi Foundation, and the foundation is now a full 501(c)(3). We waited for the negative response, but none came. One or two people asked for their money back, and we were happy to return it. But out of a total of almost $260,000 donated, over the next three months we were asked to give back only $7,000.

The other task that lay ahead of us was simpler. We wanted to do something to express our thanks to the core group of people who had helped us so much. So even though our new apartment was still half empty, and I did not have all the utensils I needed, we invited a roomfull of people over to share in a true Nigerian feast.

All day the apartment filled with the aroma of spices and cooked meat, and by the time Kayode opened the door to the first of the guests, I felt like I had been transported back in time to one of the many family gatherings that filled my childhood.

We ate well that night, and we filled the apartment with laughter too.

Pastor Phillip was there, and so were Coach Russ and Coach Shawn. Nicholas Kristof joined us, and so did Tani's principal and more than a dozen others. And as I looked around at them all, Jews and Muslims, nonbelievers and Christians, it struck me that even though our story started with hatred and division, it was now about unity.

As I mingled and laughed and talked with our guests, so many of their words stayed with me.

"I've been writing for a long time," said Nicholas. "But I've never seen anything like it. No news lasts more than twenty-four hours in America. But this story just kept on going."

"Your son has been an angel in my life," said Coach Shawn.

"People want a counter to all the negativity these days," said Coach Russ. "And that's what Tani's story does. It reminds us that good is stronger than evil, that we *can* be kind, that we *can* be generous, that people *do* care. It's the American dream all over, a reminder that this country was built for good. It shows that God exists, and I really believe that the idea of Tani can create a positive change in this world."

I remembered the article that I read about Coach Shawn in the *New York Times*. Right at the end it described the way he approached chess, saying that he played in an aggressive style and liked to use his pawns as attackers.

"When you put pawns together, there's no stopping them," he said. "You put two or three together and they practically control the whole game."[7]

Looking around the apartment that night, I could see there were some powerful people, men and women with fame and influence in the world.

But there were others, too, the kind of people who don't have great wealth or great recognition. Immigrants, people who worked hard, educators, and pastors. People who go quietly about their lives, just moving forward day by day. People like Kayode and me.

In other words, pawns.

I thought about all those small gifts to the campaign. What can five dollars buy you? What change can ten dollars make in the world? Not much, it would seem. But put them together with the generosity of four thousand other people, and these dollars can add up to something significant.

That's how miracles happen.

ACKNOWLEDGMENTS

This book would not exist without the help of so many different people.

Years before the world showed its generosity to us in such a dramatic way in New York, our family back in Nigeria demonstrated its love and support of us. We will forever be grateful for the kindness and care of Prince Joseph Oba Adewumi and Mrs. Jaiye Florence Adewumi, the late Alhaji Jimoh Afolabi Owoeye and Mrs. Funke Adenike Owoeye, the late Felix Akinboboye, as well as so many siblings, uncles and aunts, and friends.

The Nigerian community in New York has also showed love, and we are particularly grateful to Mr. and Mrs. Femi Ajayi and Pastor Phillip Taye Falayi. They invited us in when we had nowhere to go.

We are particularly grateful to Principal Jane Hsu and Kyrie Gilmore, Tani's third grade teacher at P.S. 116 in New York. Together with the rest of the staff, they have helped us all in so many ways.

PATH DHS Assessment Shelter in the Bronx found us a place to live when we were in need, and the staff at the shelter on Park Avenue treated all of us with kindness.

There have been so many people who have helped us with our legal case, and our immigration attorneys (Heather Volik and Carolina Curbelo) and family attorney (Shamsey Oloko) have given us excellent help.

We are grateful for the opportunity to share this story like this and thank our agent Cait Hoyt and her assistant, Lili Cohen, and Michelle

Weiner and her assistant, Abby Walters, at Creative Artists Agency for their guidance, wisdom, and continued help. Matt Baugher, Daisy Hutton, Beth Adams, and the team at HarperCollins who have worked so hard to produce this book, and we are grateful, too, for the help of our writer, Craig Borlase. Thanks are due also to Paramount Film Production for all that they are doing to bring this story to life.

We have been blessed by the support of some remarkable people who treated us with such dignity. For a family of asylum seekers to be invited to visit President Bill Clinton was so special. But to see him and Tani talk with such passion about their interests was astounding. Nicholas Kristof at the *New York Times* was instrumental in sharing our story, and we still marvel at the way he inspired so many readers and ignited a fire that spread to the media across the whole world.

This story would not exist without chess, and Tani has been supported so well by the United States Chess Federation and Saint Louis Chess Club. But there would be no chess for Tani if not for the patience, the generosity, and the inspiration of Coach Shawn Martinez and Coach Russell Makofsky. They are mighty men to whom we owe a great debt of gratitude. We thank them from the bottom of our hearts.

Last of all, we would like to thank the thousands of people from all over the world who donated to our GoFundMe campaign as well as those who gave us a car, awards, a place to live, and all the things we needed to fill our apartment. Together you changed our world. Now we hope to change the world for others.

Kayode, Oluwatoyin, Austin, and Tani
New York, New York, December 2019

NOTES

1. Nicholas Kristof, "This 8-Year-Old Chess Champion Will Make You Smile," *New York Times*, March 16, 2019, https://www.nytimes.com/2019/03/16/opinion/sunday/chess-champion-8-year-old-homeless-refugee-.html.
2. Traveling Wilbury, March 16, 2019, comment on Kristof, "This 8-Year-Old Chess Champion."
3. Joe Wolf, March 16, 2019, comment on Kristof, "This 8-Year-Old Chess Champion."
4. Another Voice, March 16, 2019, comment on Kristof, "This 8-Year-Old Chess Champion."
5. Russell Makofsky in Kayode Adewumi (organizer), "Just Tani," GoFundMe (web page), March 15, 2019, https://www.gofundme.com/f/just-tani.
6. Nicholas Kristof, "Our Chess Champion Has a New Home," *New York Times*, March 23, 2019, https://www.nytimes.com/2019/03/23/opinion/sunday/homeless-chess-champion-tani.html.
7. Timothy Williams, "Teenage Riddle: Skipping Class, Mastering Chess," *New York Times,* April 13, 2007, https://www.nytimes.com/2007/04/13/nyregion/13chess.html.

ABOUT THE AUTHORS

TANITOLUWA "TANI" ADEWUMI is the Nigerian-born boy who won the New York State chess championship after playing the game for only a year. After Tani and his family fled Nigeria amid Boko Haram's reign of terror, they found refuge in a New York City homeless shelter, where they waited to be granted religious asylum. Tani's father, **Kayode Adewumi**, who came from a royal Nigerian family, became a dishwasher and an Uber driver to support their family. **Oluwatoyin Adewumi**, Tani's mother, whose father was an accountant at one of the largest printing presses in Nigeria and who had been working at a bank for more than a decade, trained to become a home health aide. Their lives were forever changed when a chess instructor at Tani's school offered Tani a scholarship to join the chess program.

CRAIG BORLASE is a bestselling British author and collaborative writer of more than forty-five books. He specializes in memoir, and his most recent books include the *New York Times* bestseller *Finding Gobi* by Dion Leonard and *God's Hostage* by Andrew Brunson.